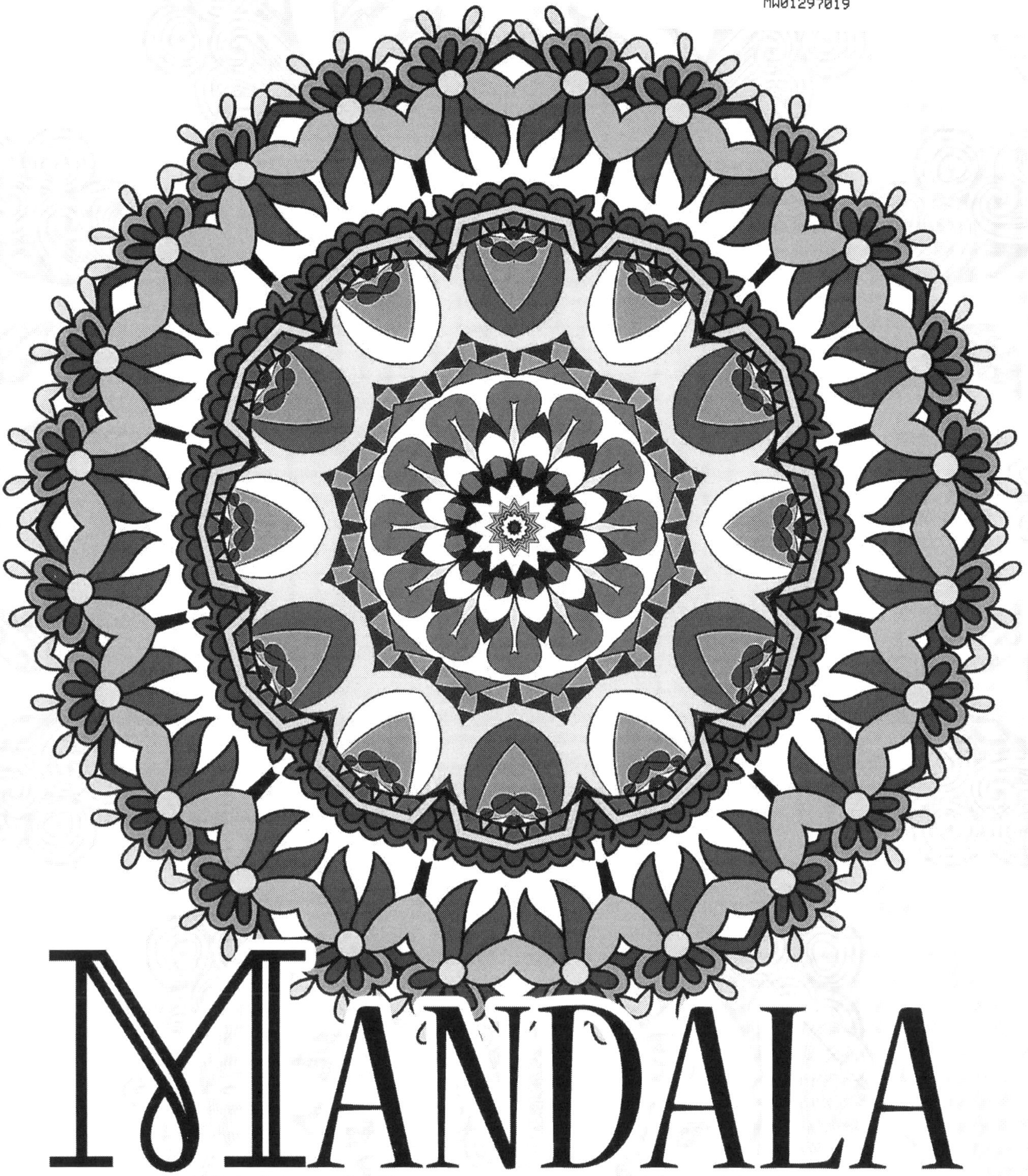

MANDALA

MEDITATION

COLORING BOOKS FOR ADULTS

STRESS RELIEVING PATTERNS

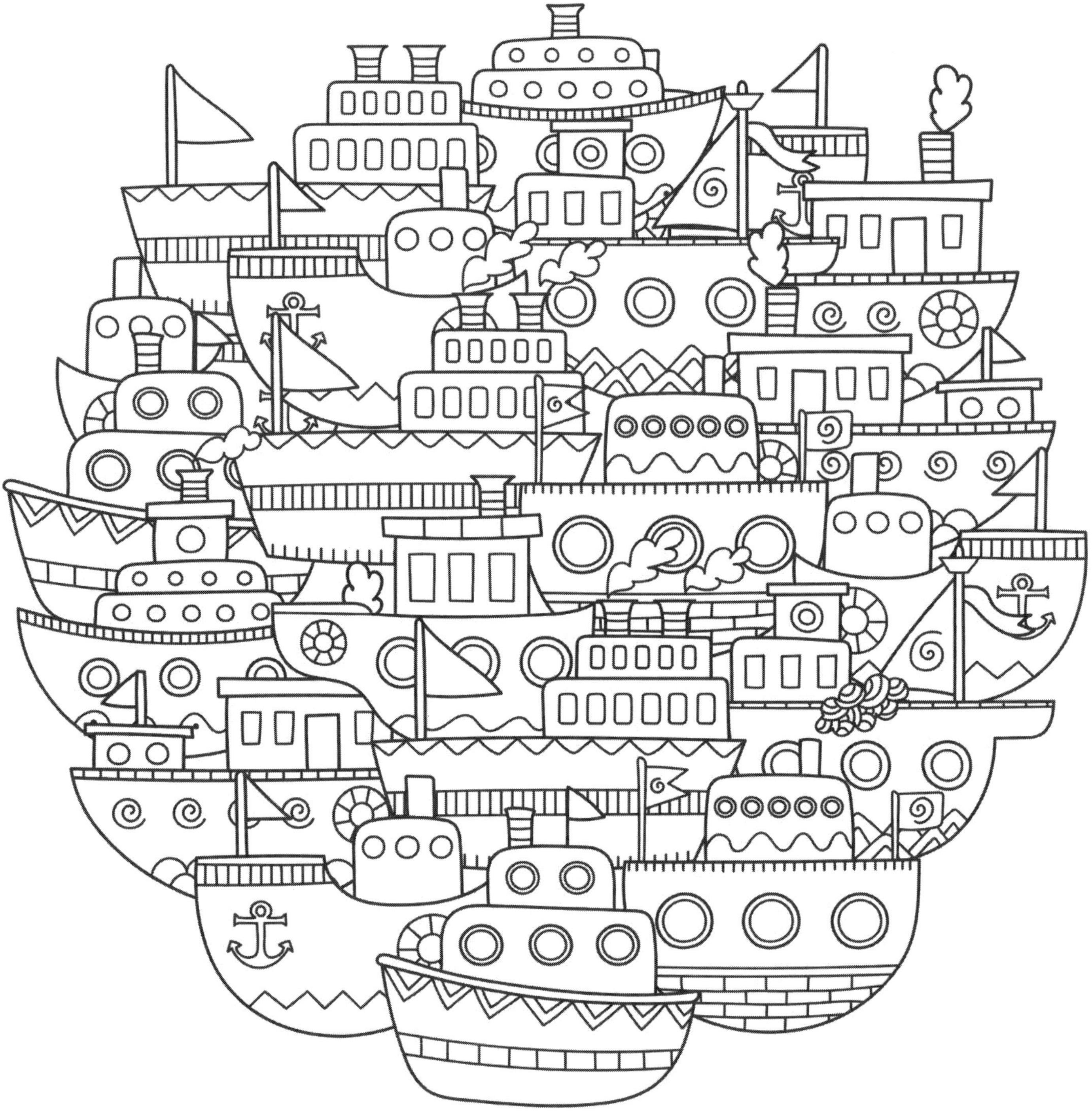

TEST YOUR COLOR

TEST YOUR COLOR

1.

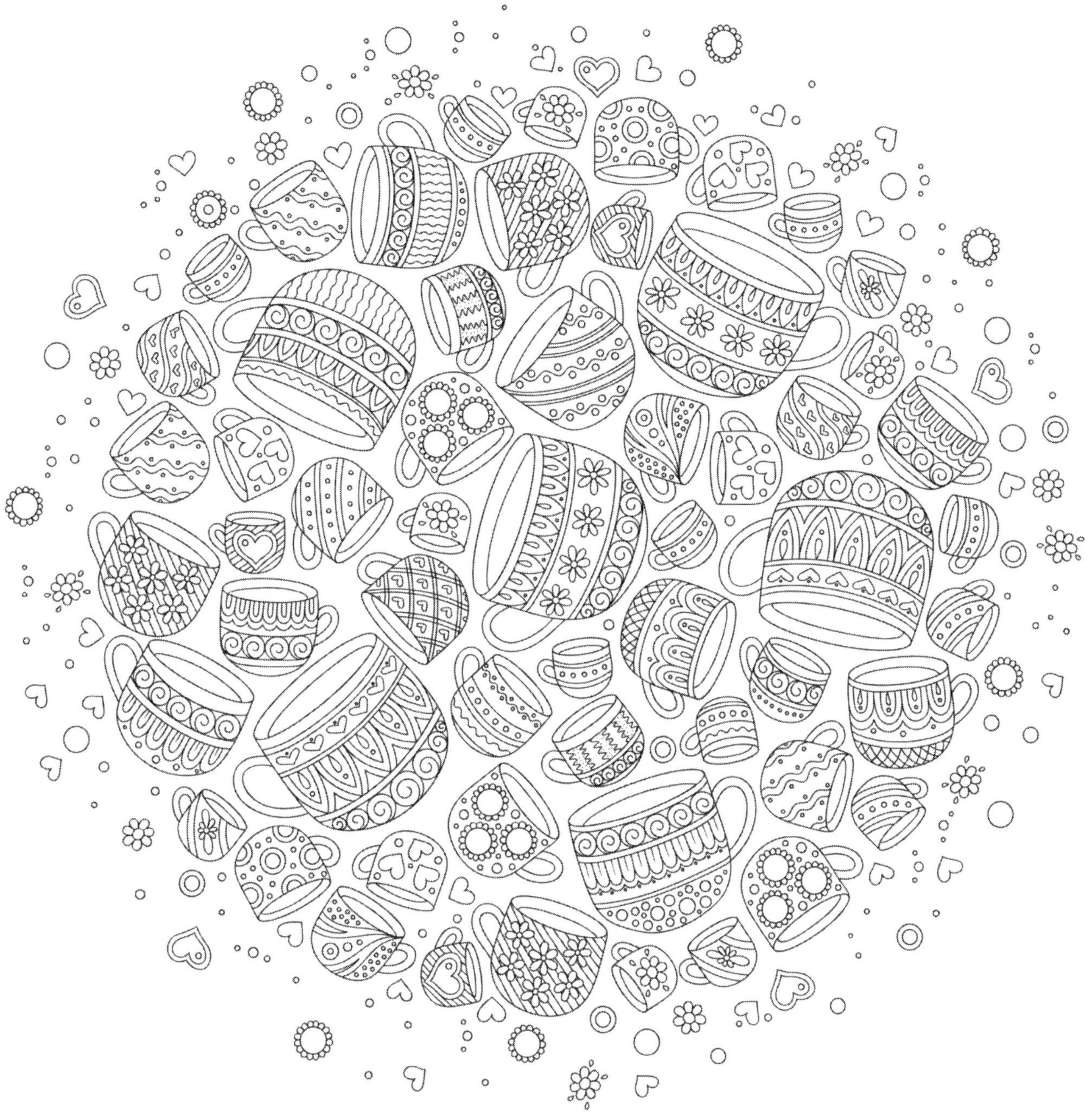

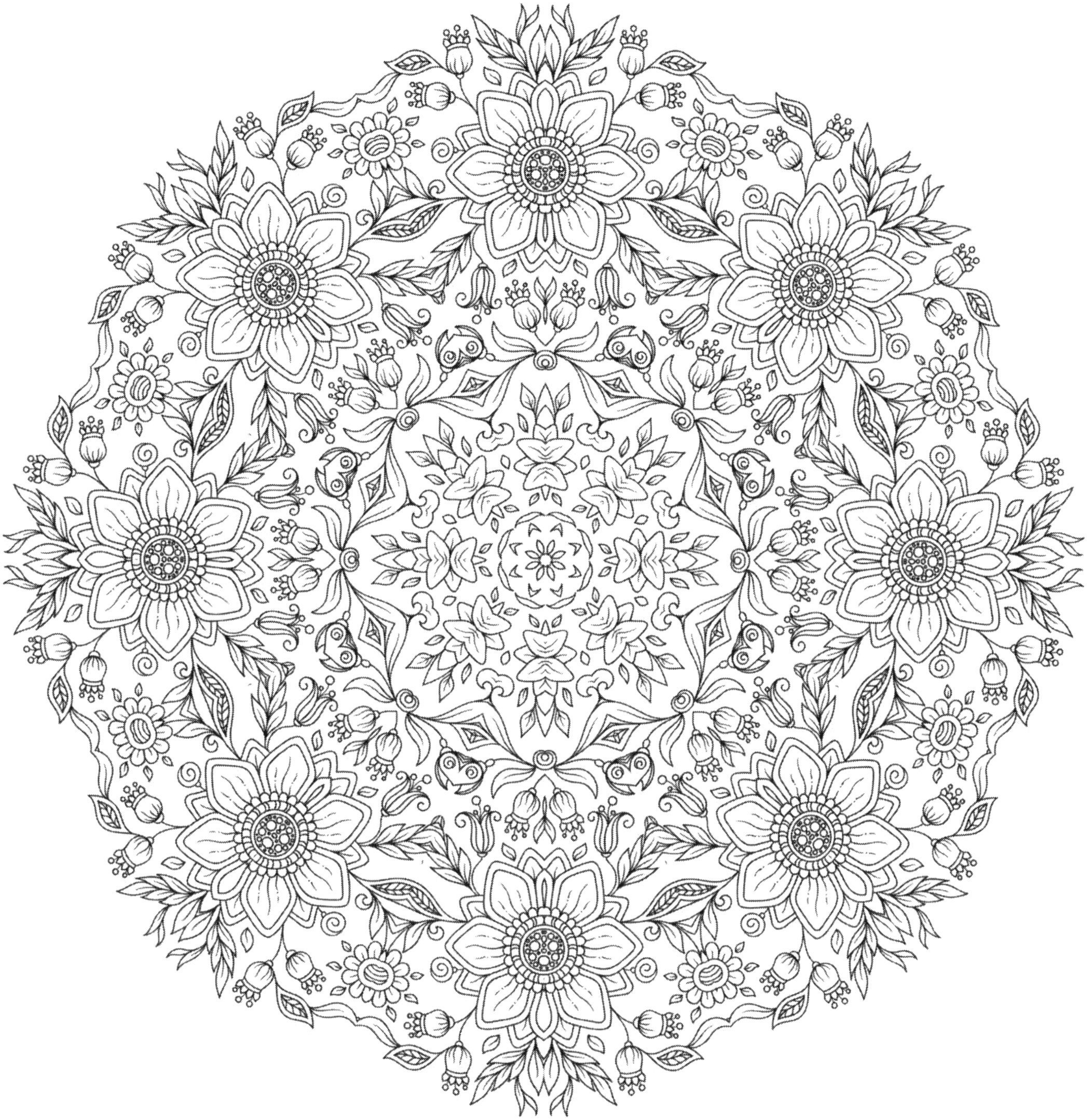

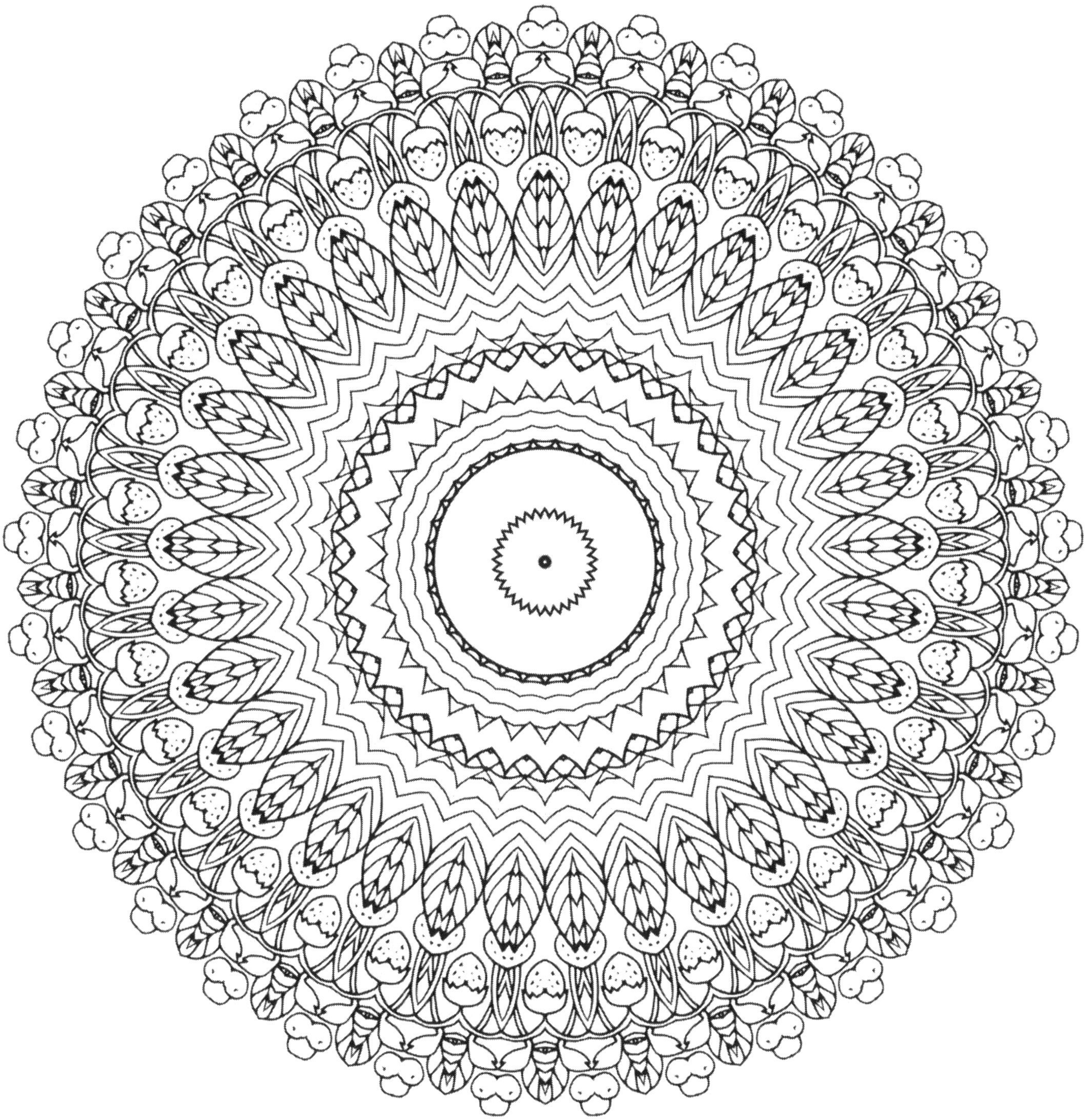

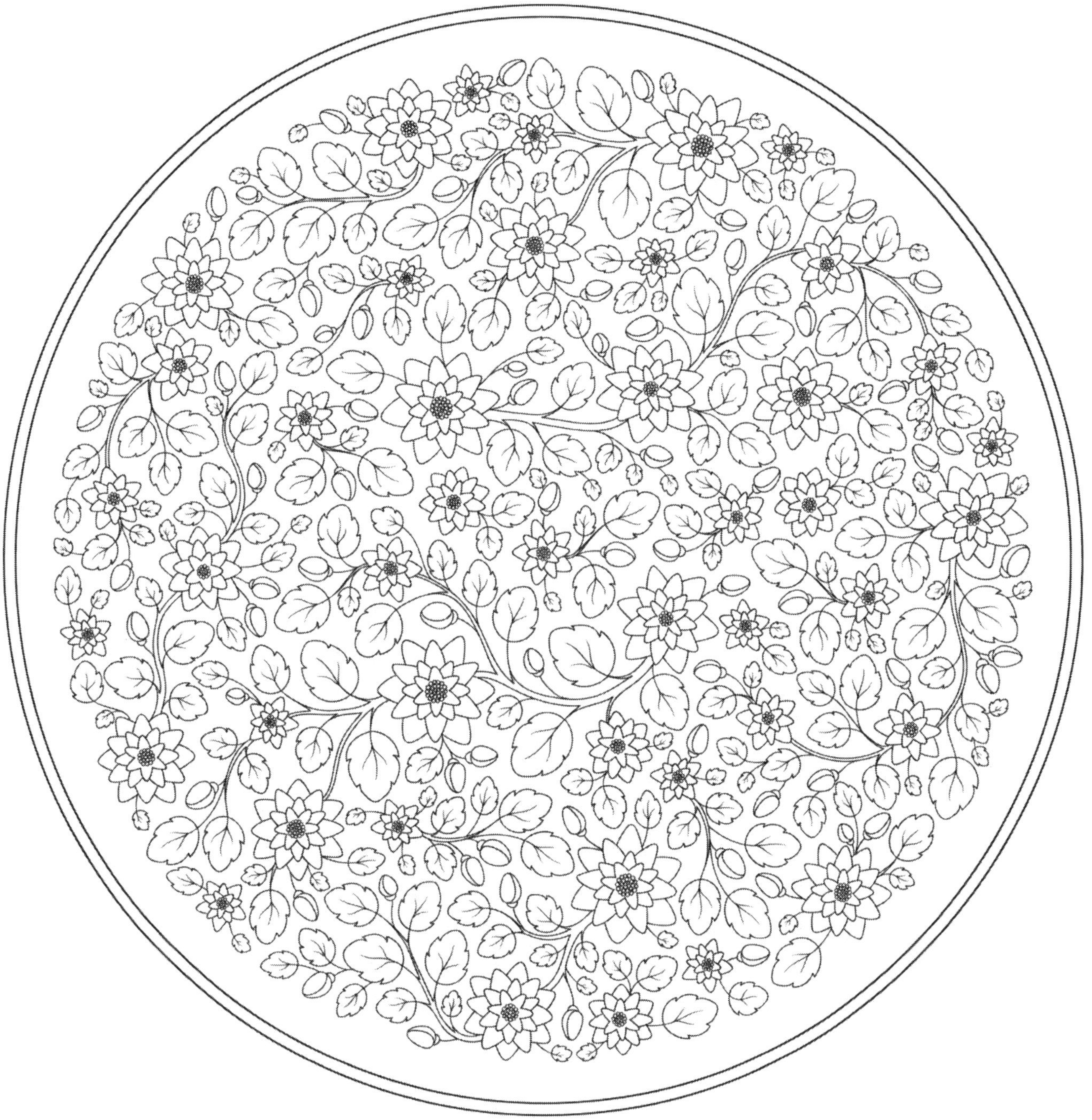

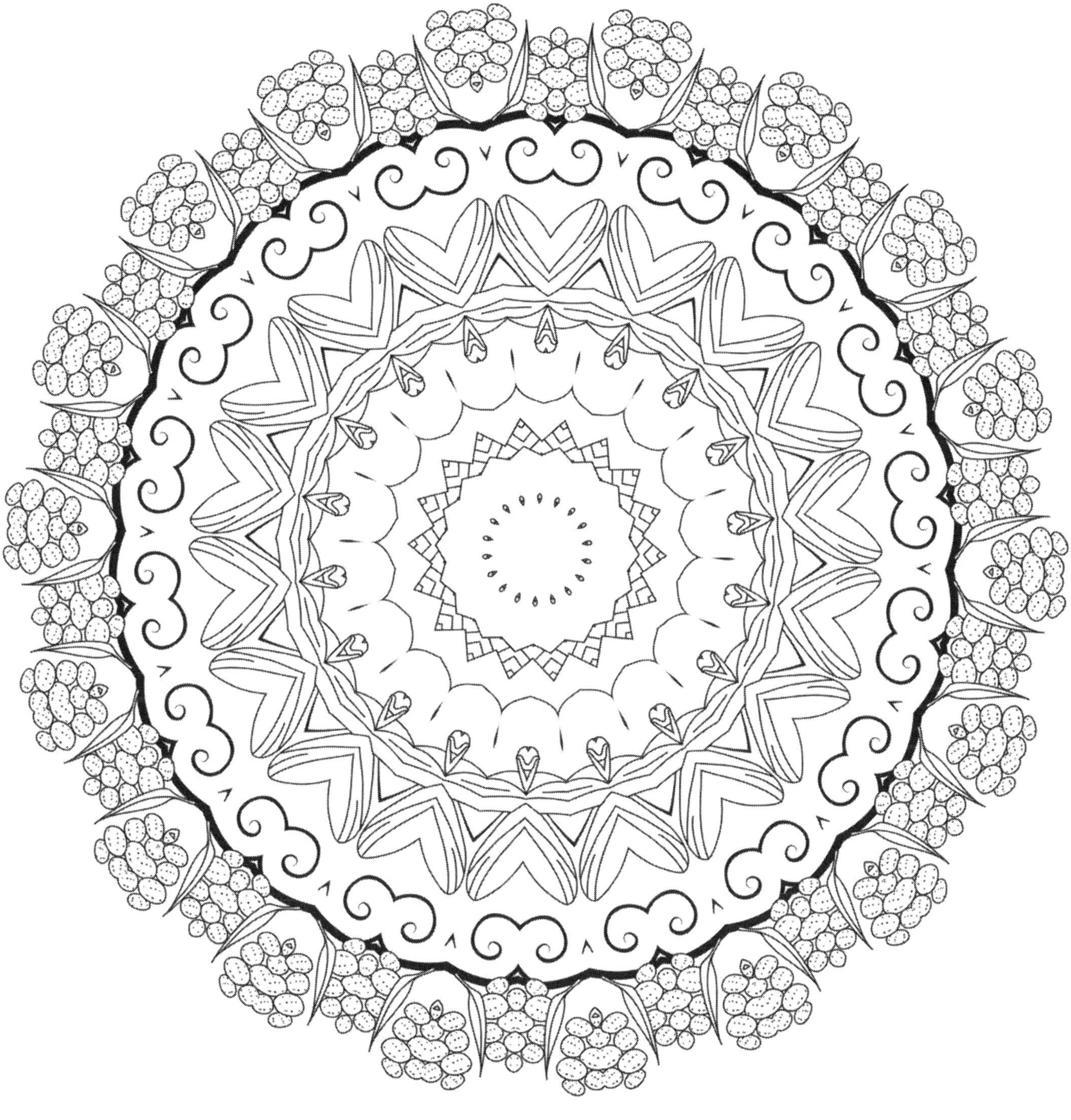

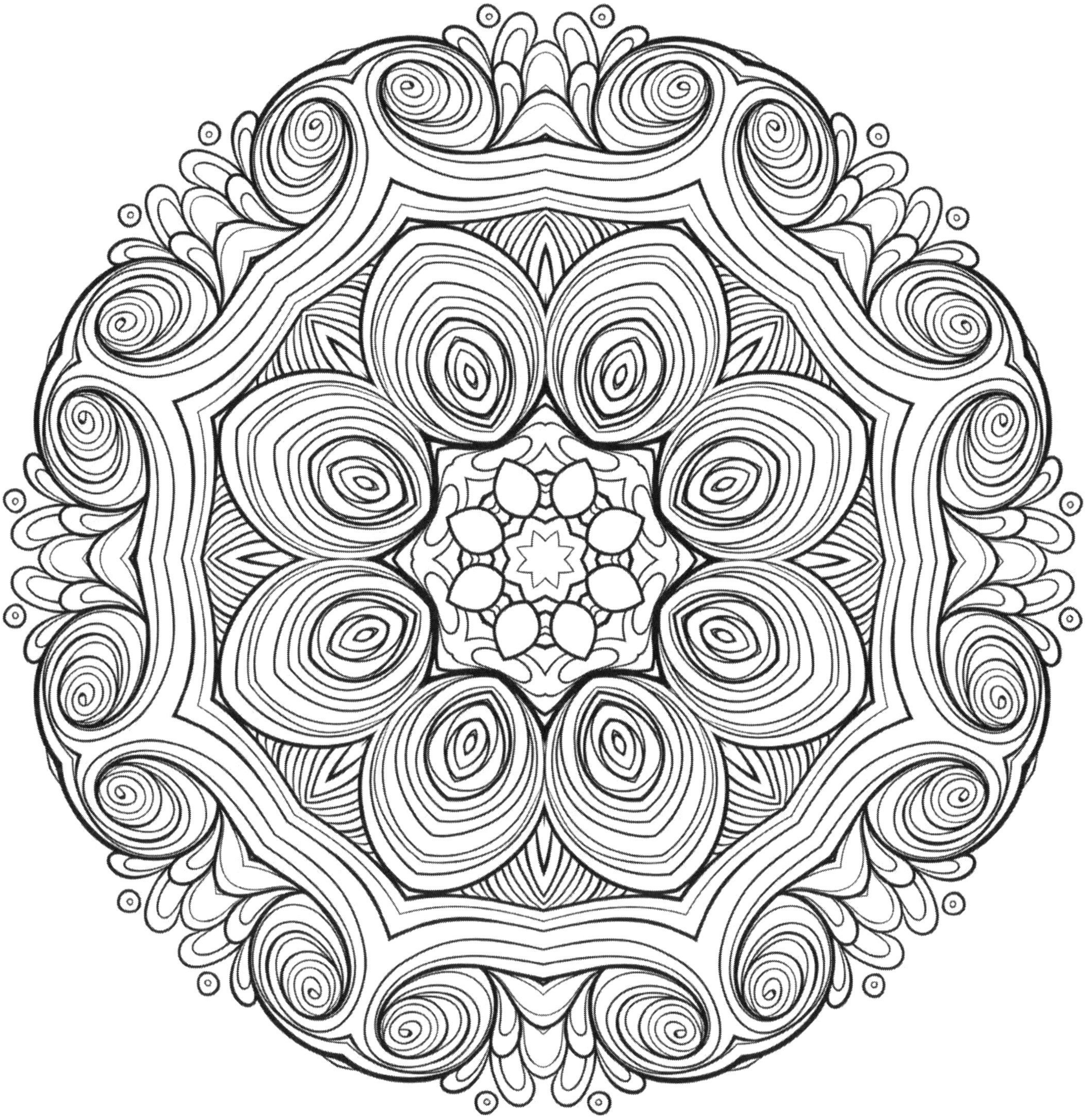

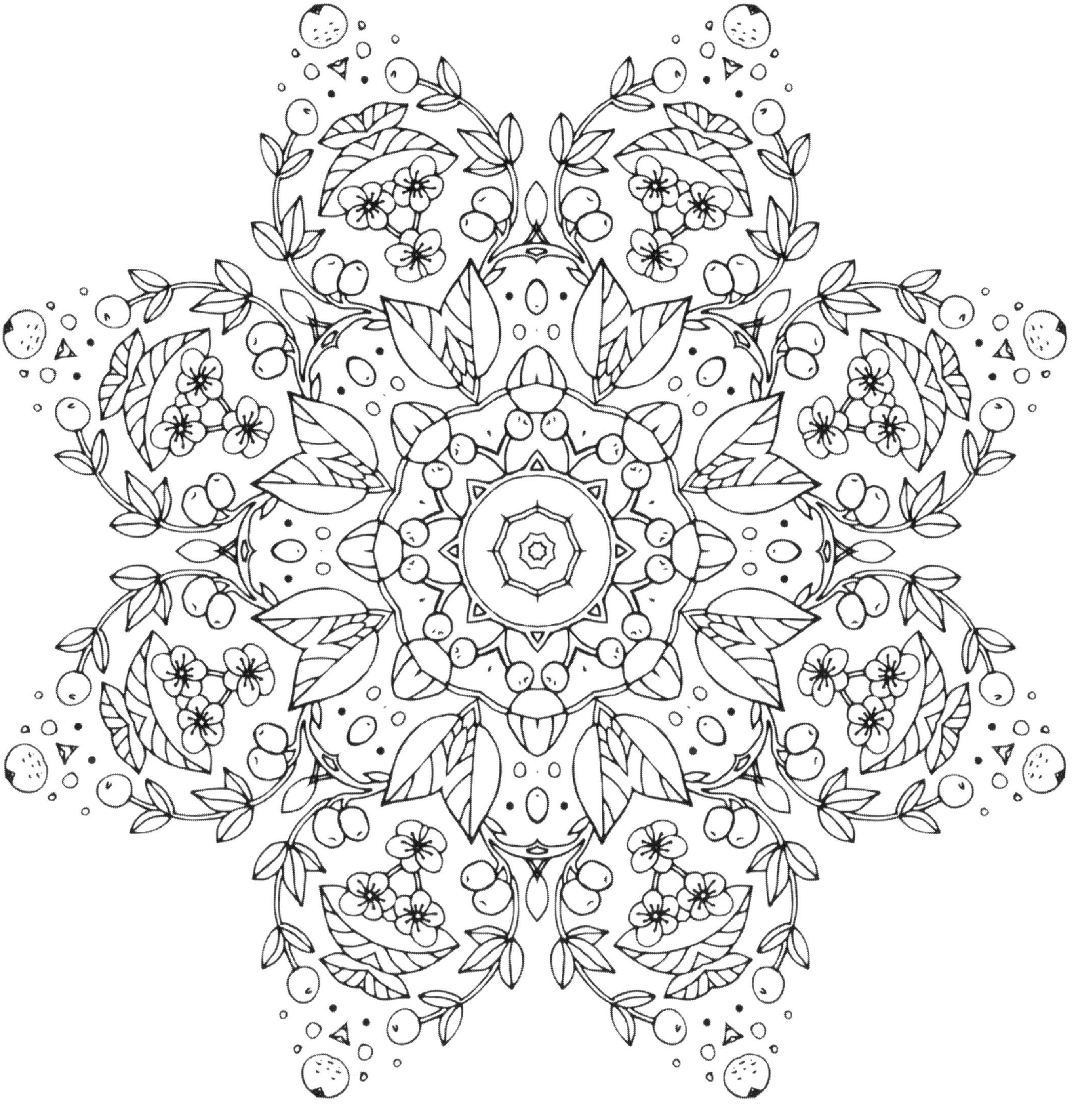

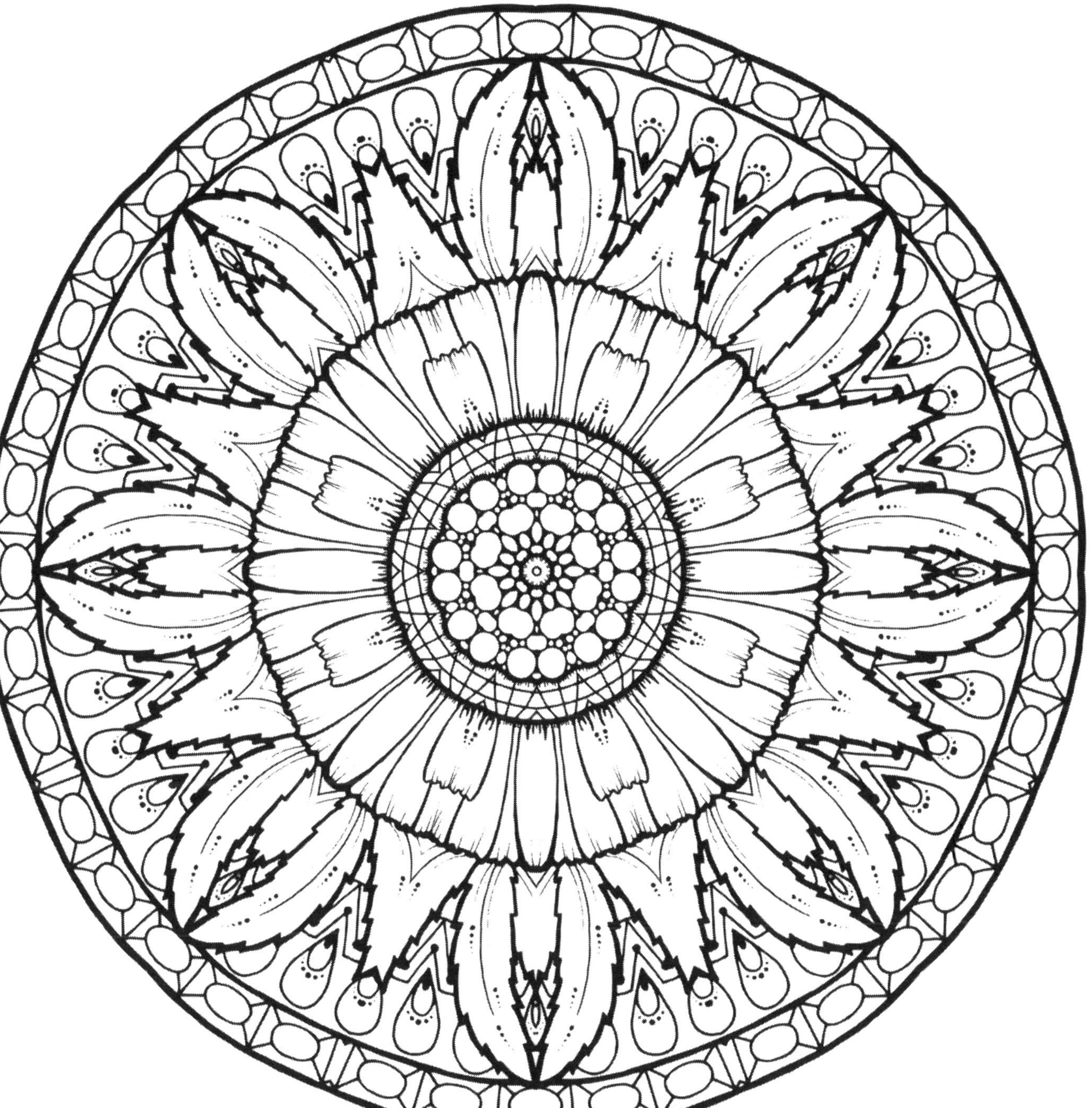

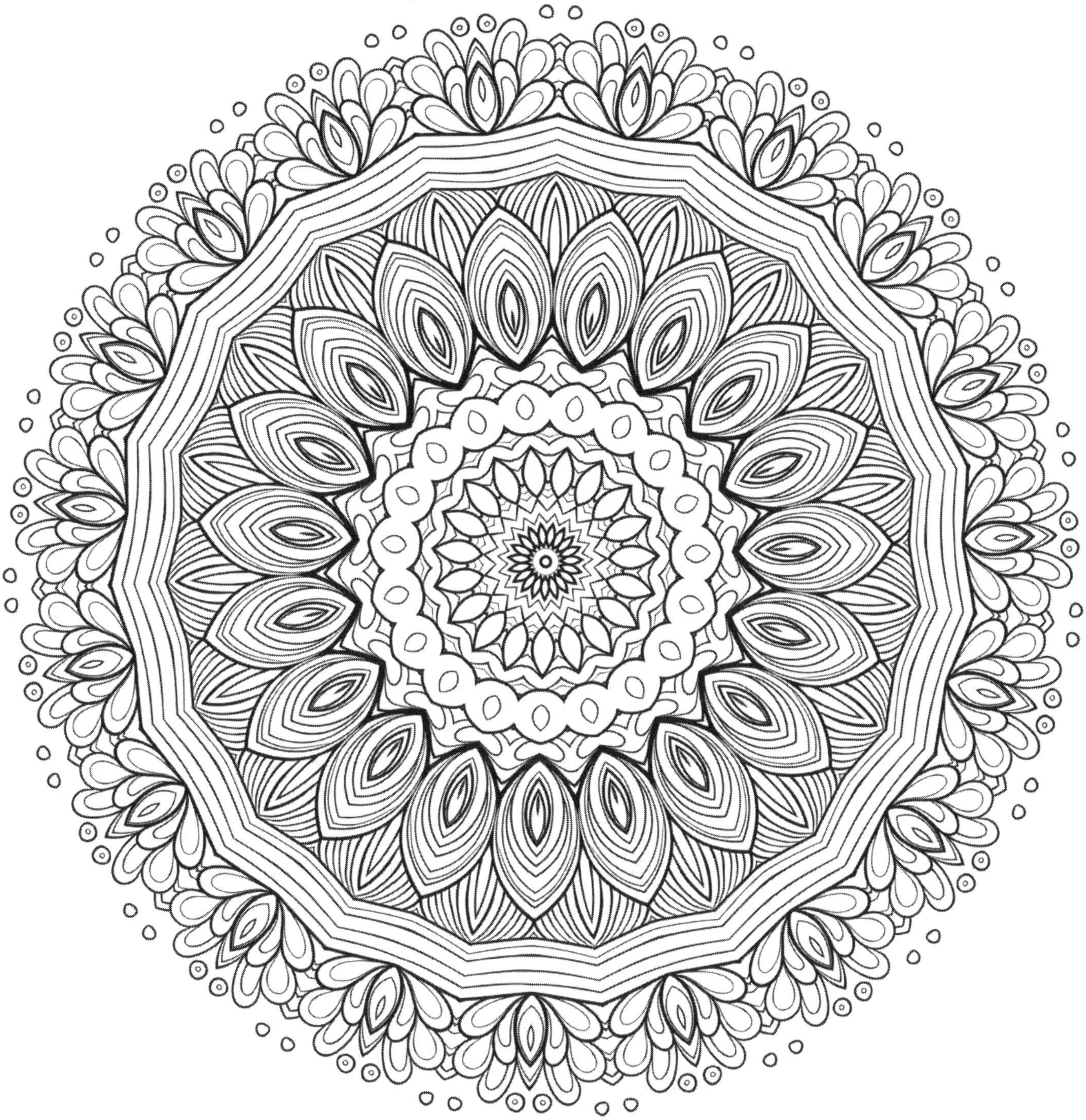

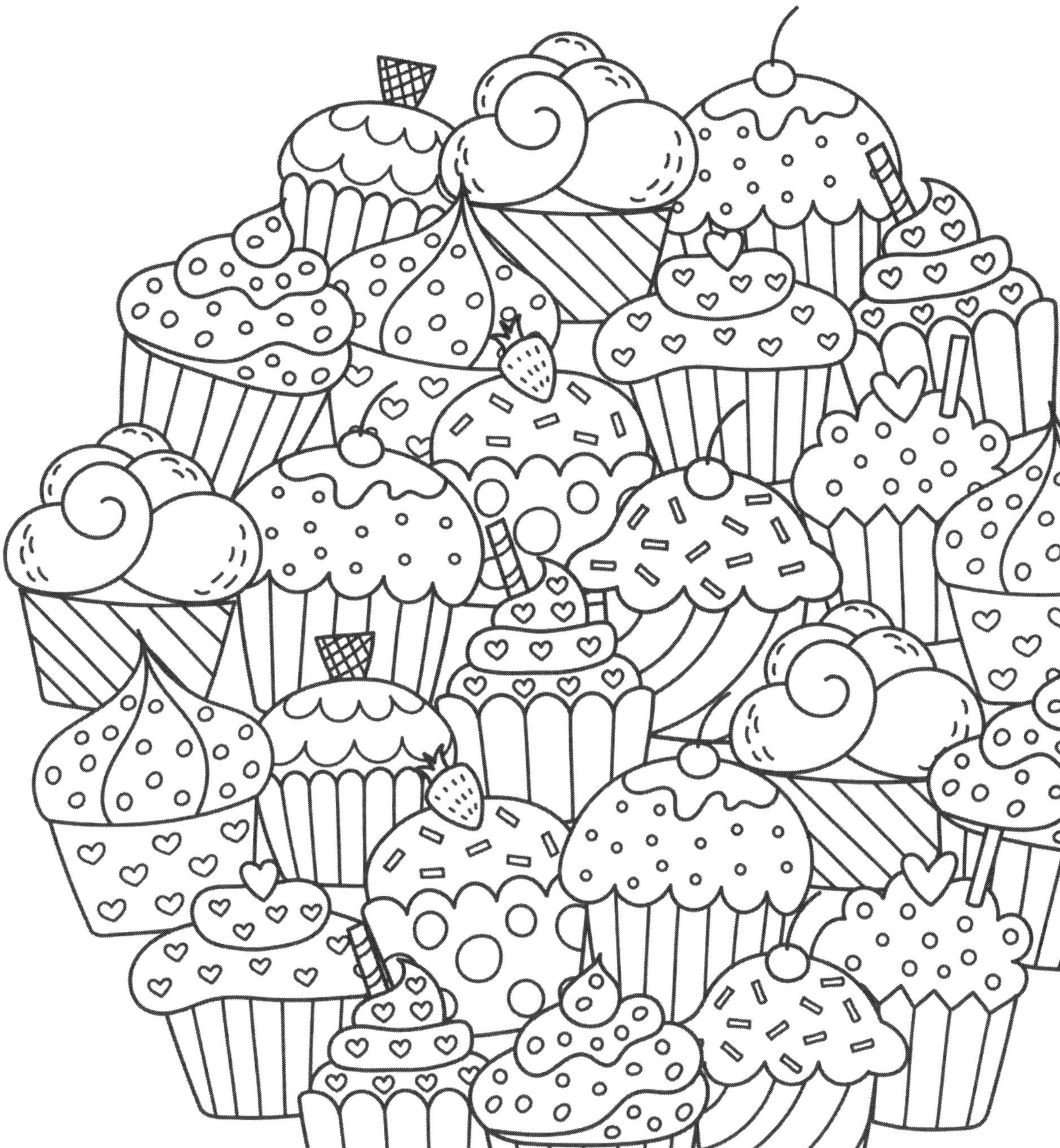

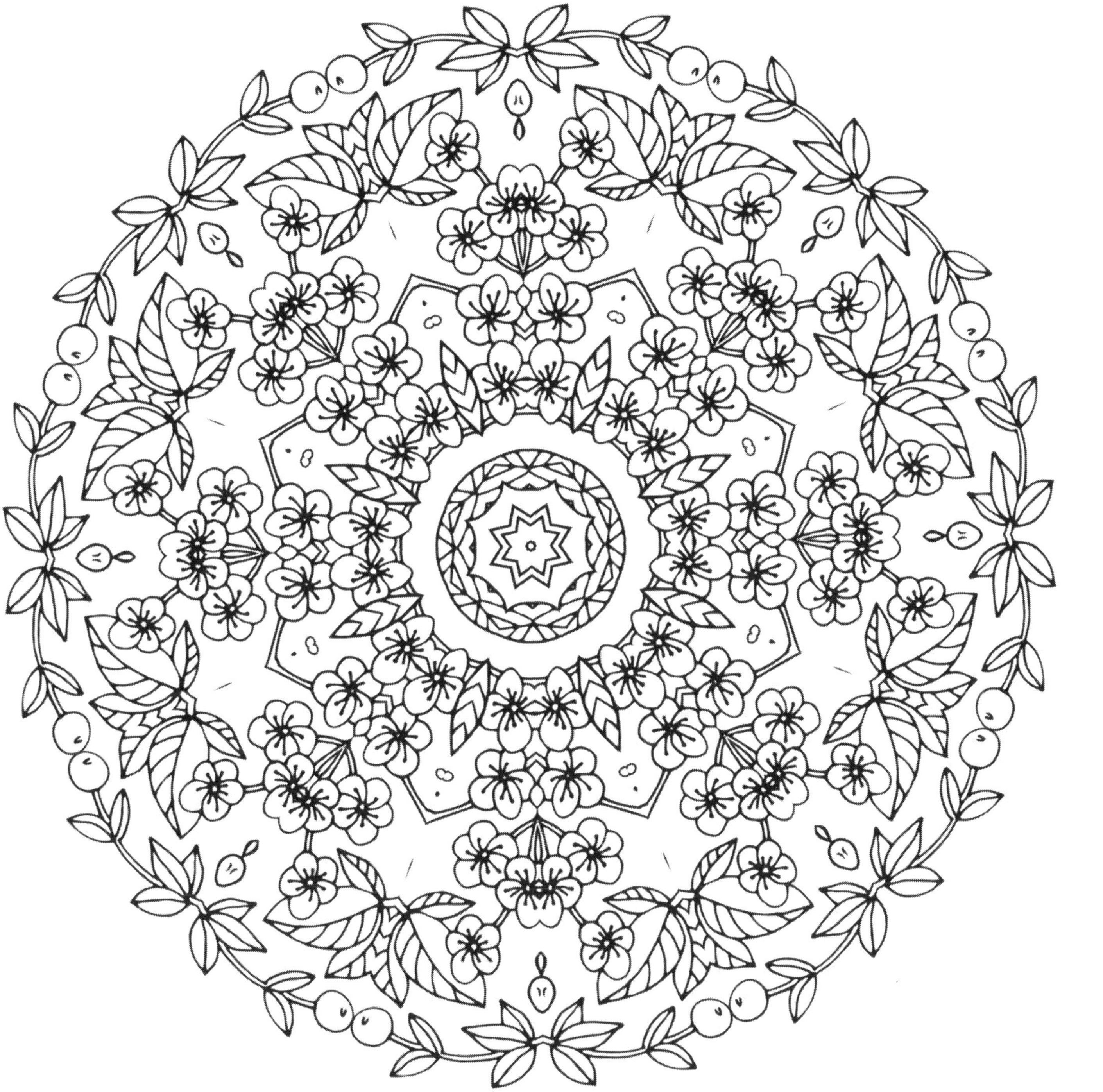

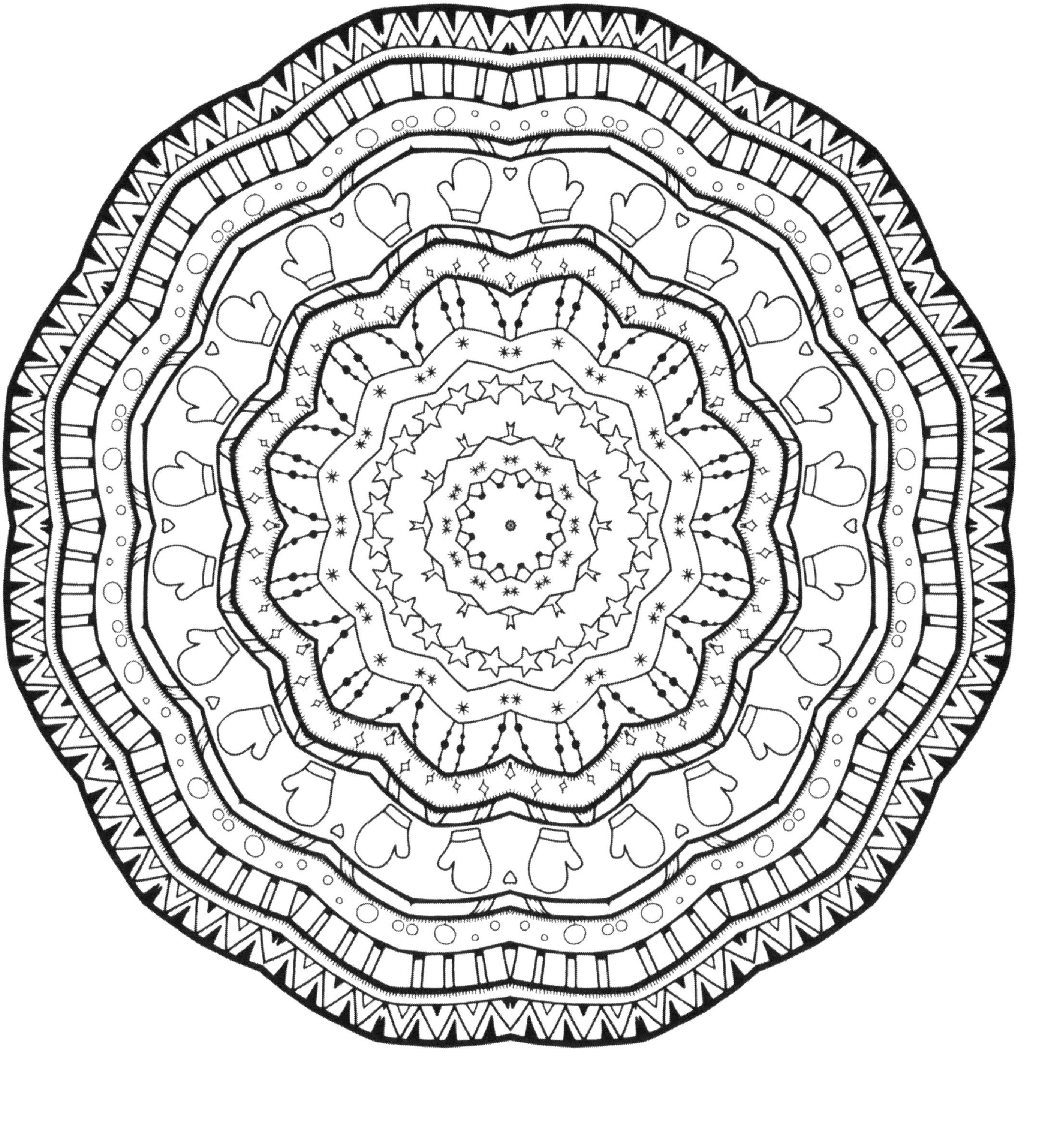

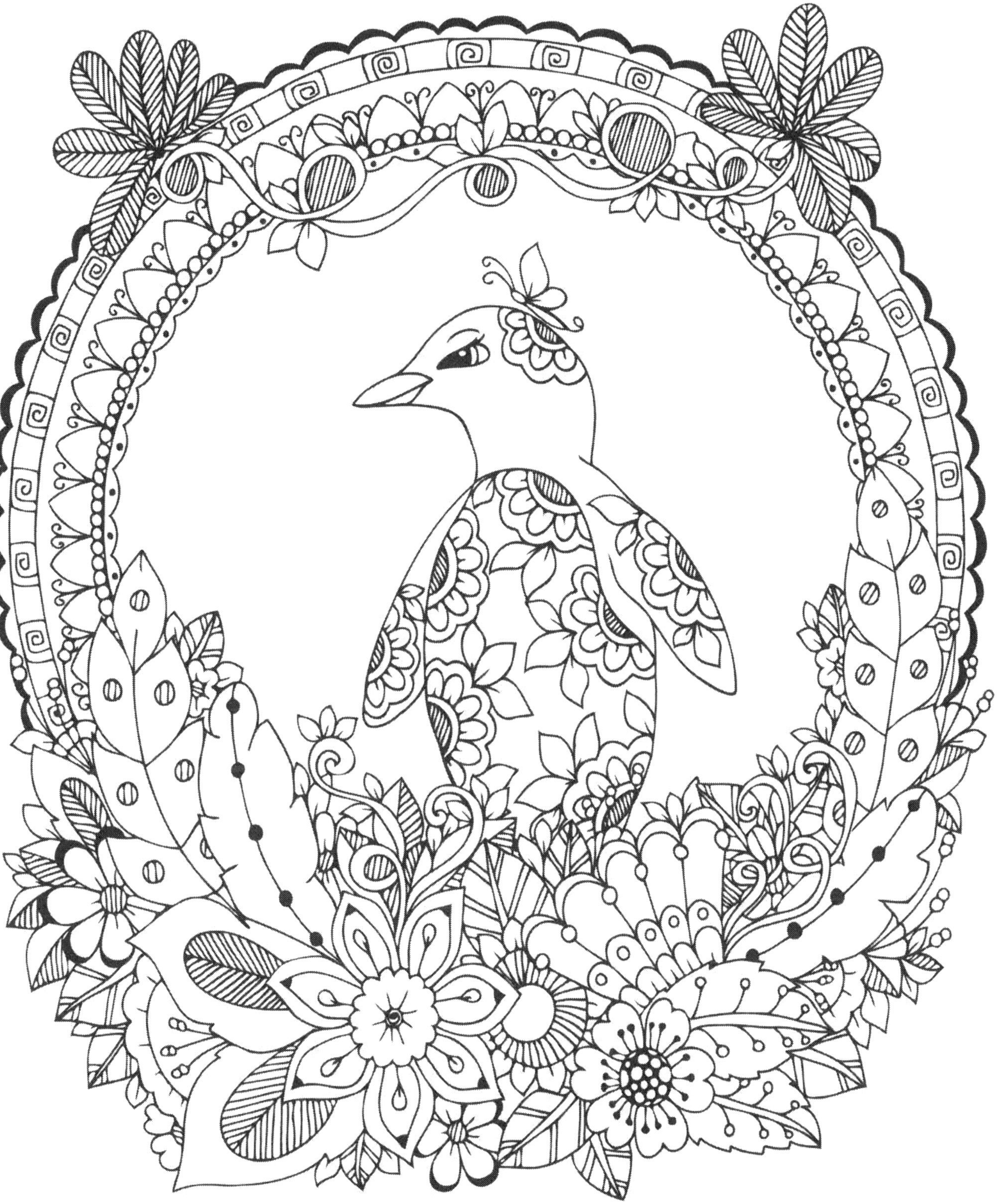

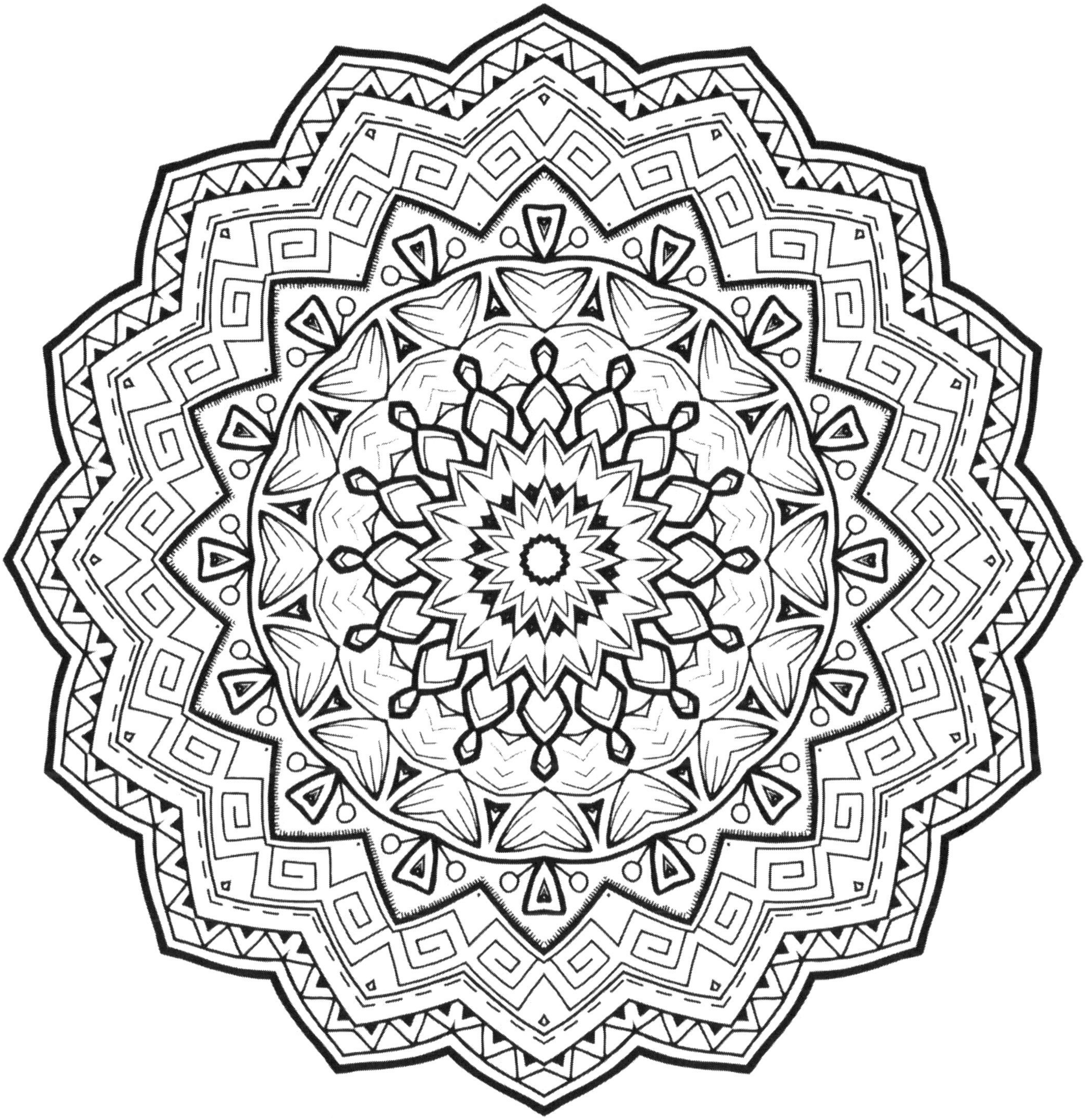

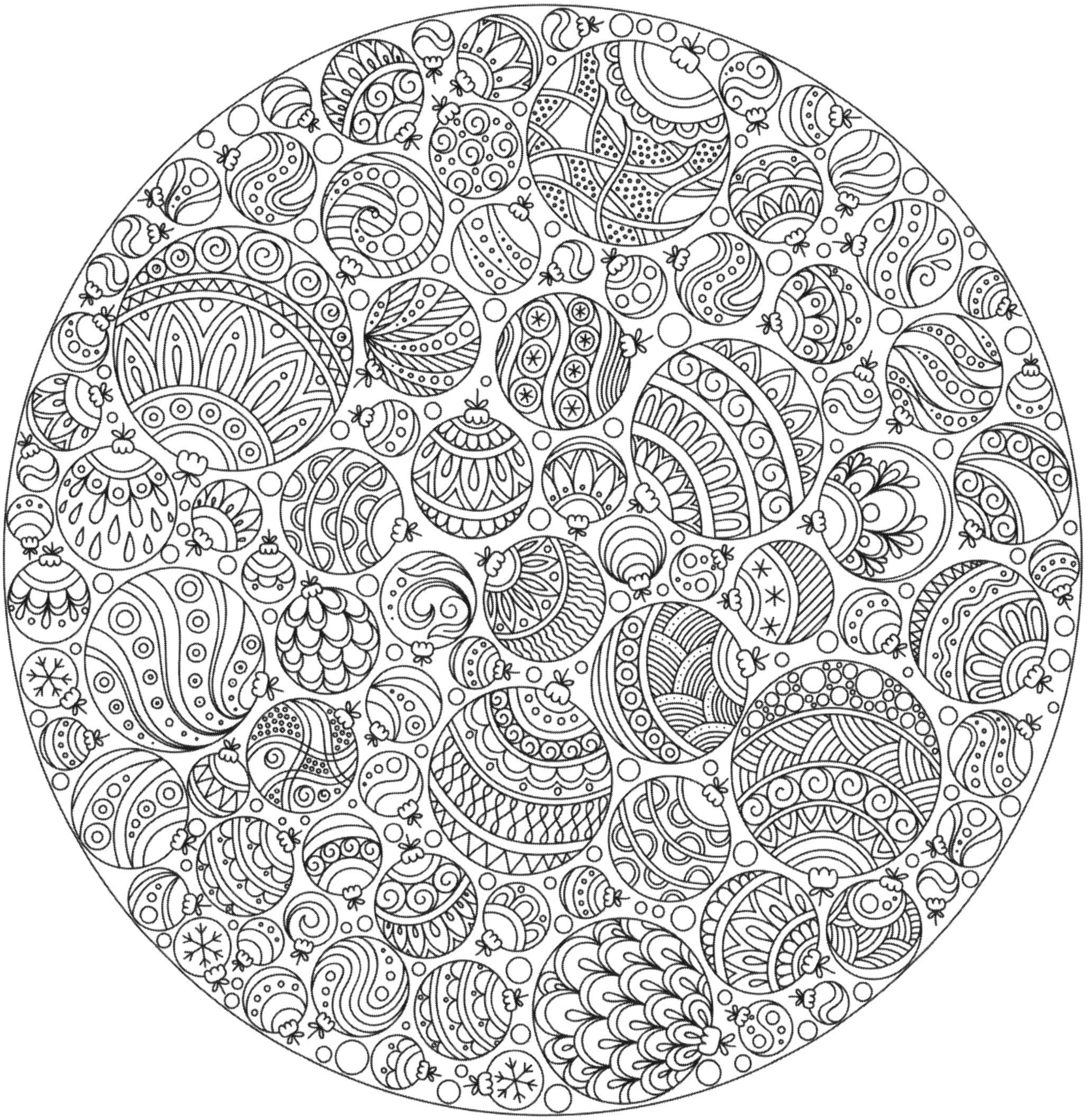

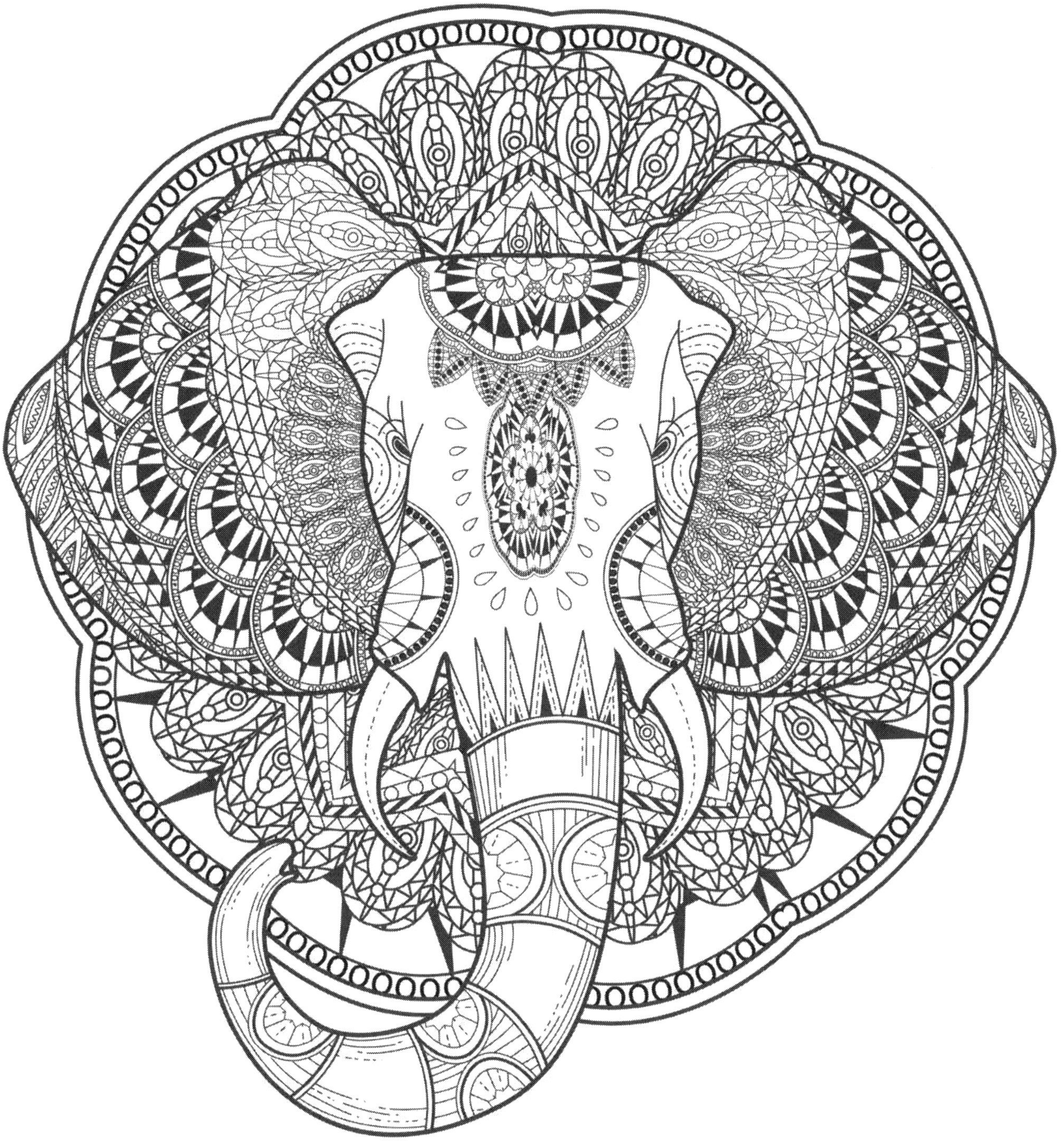

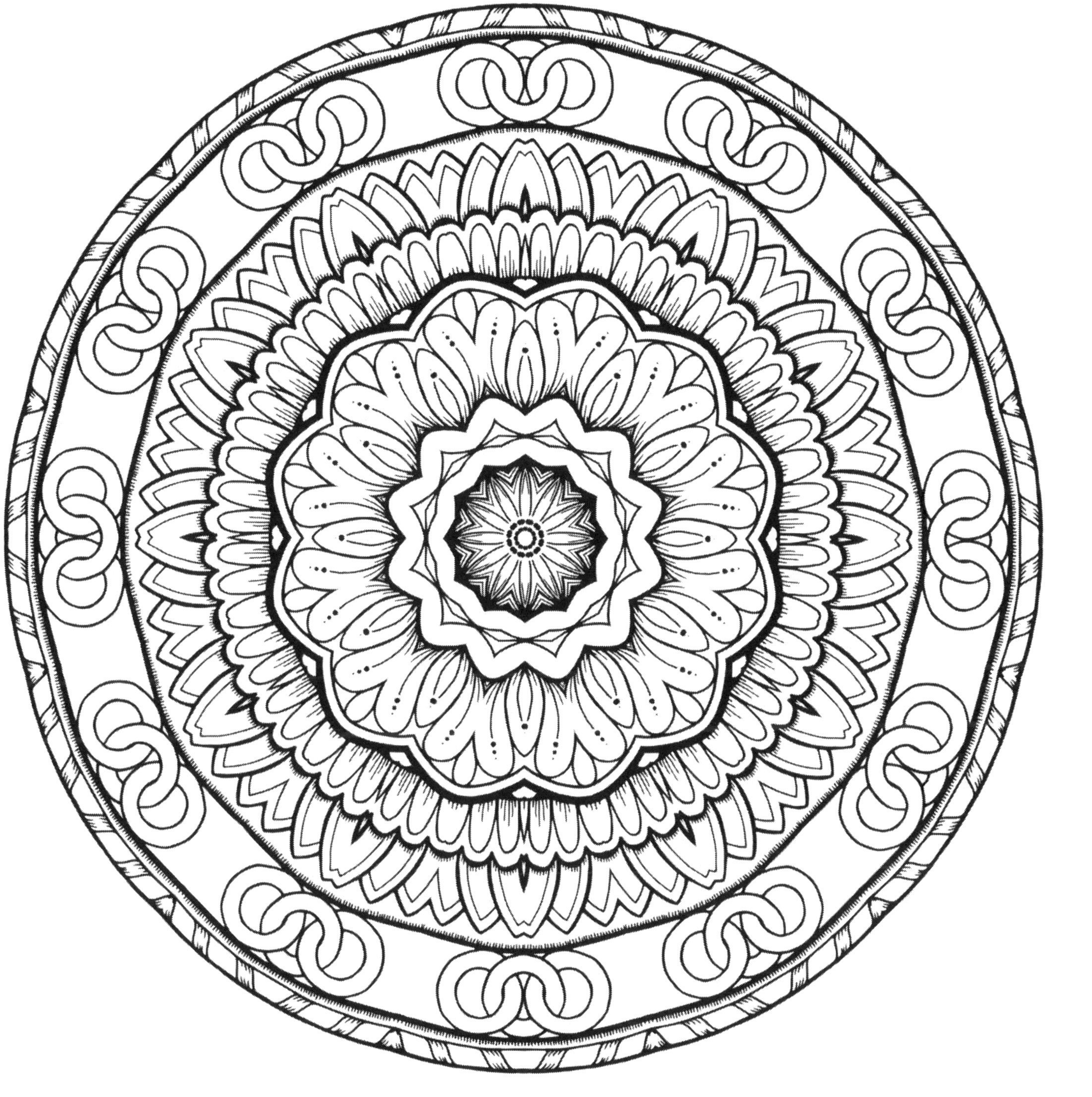

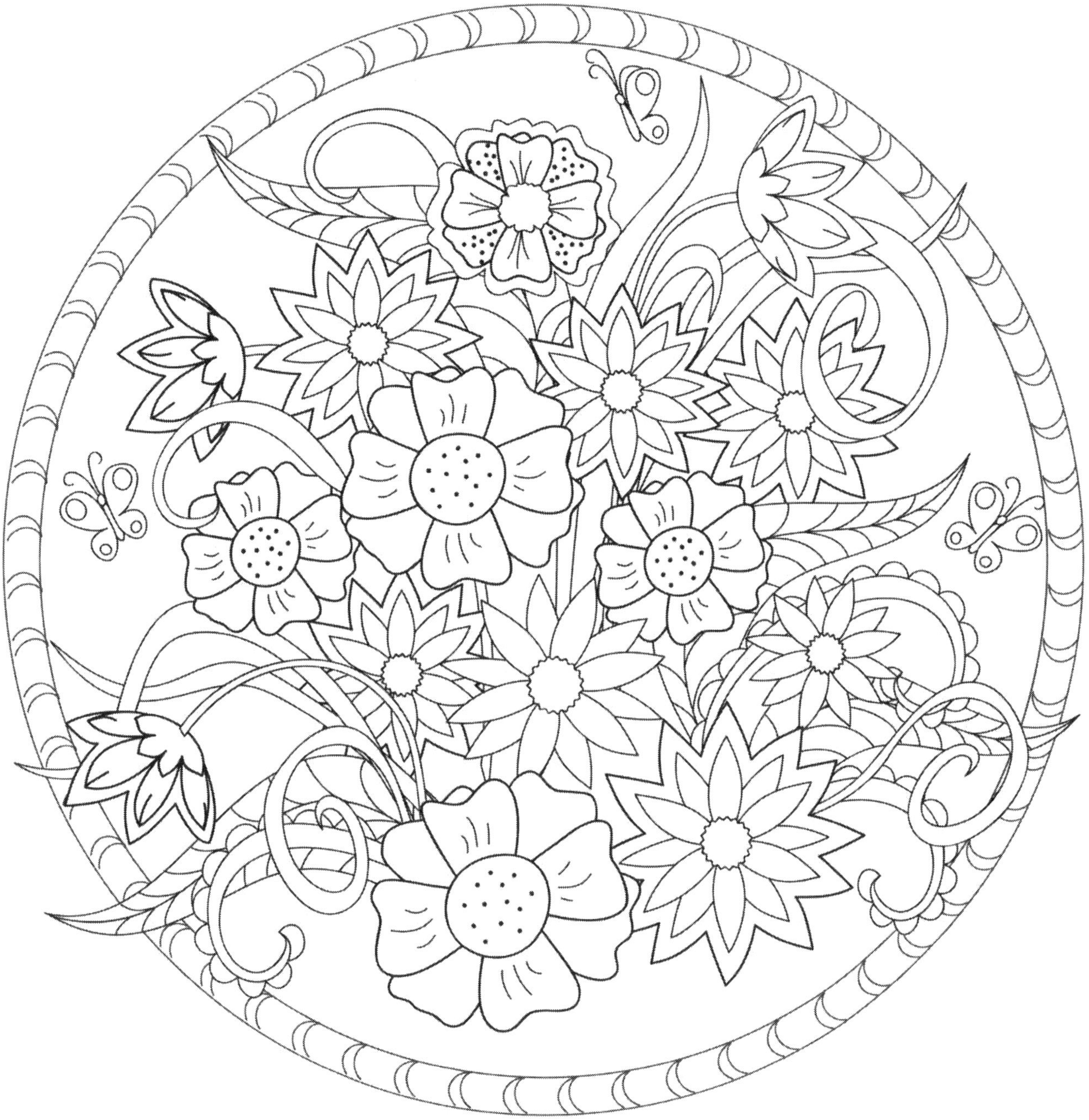

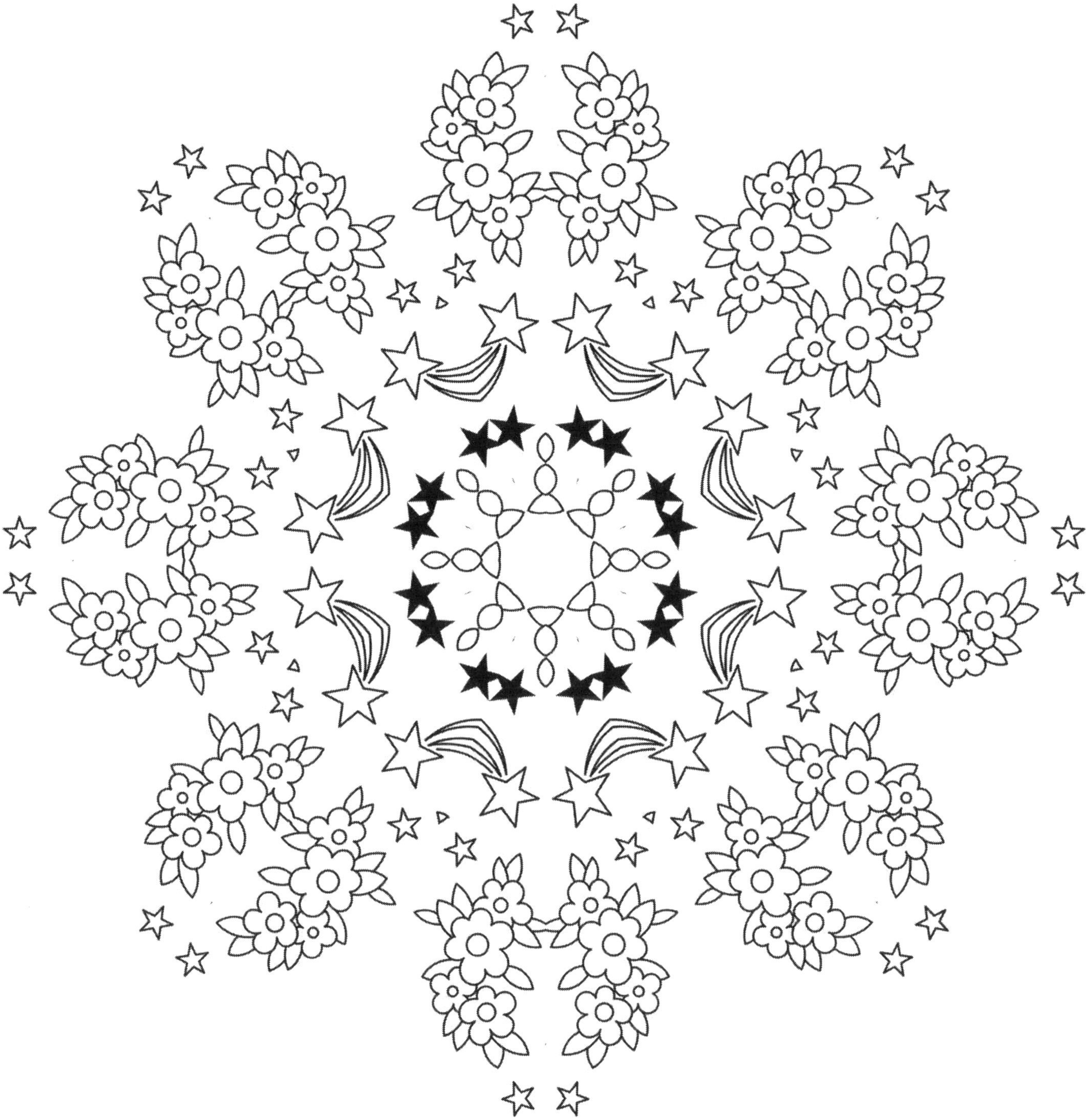

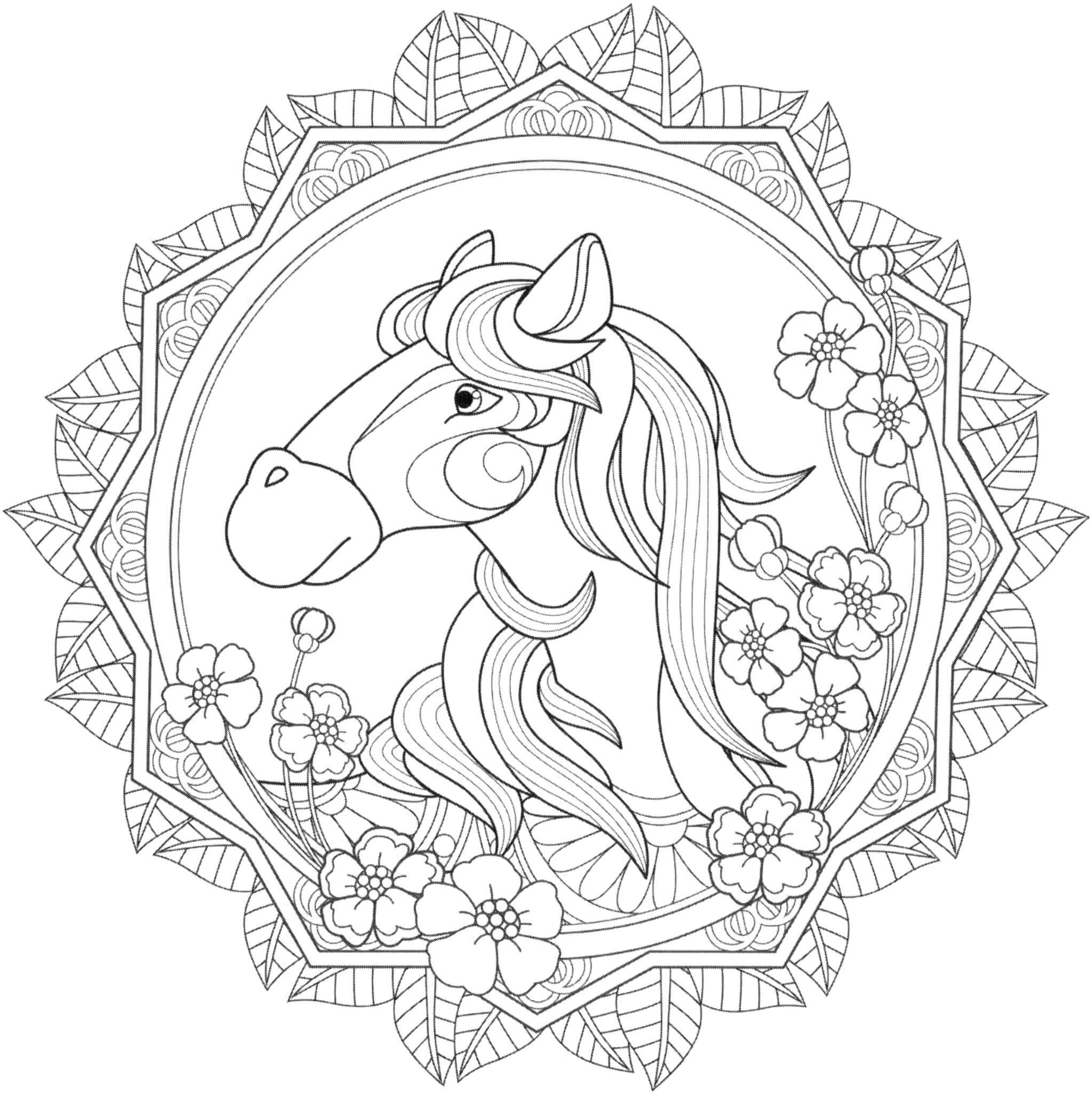

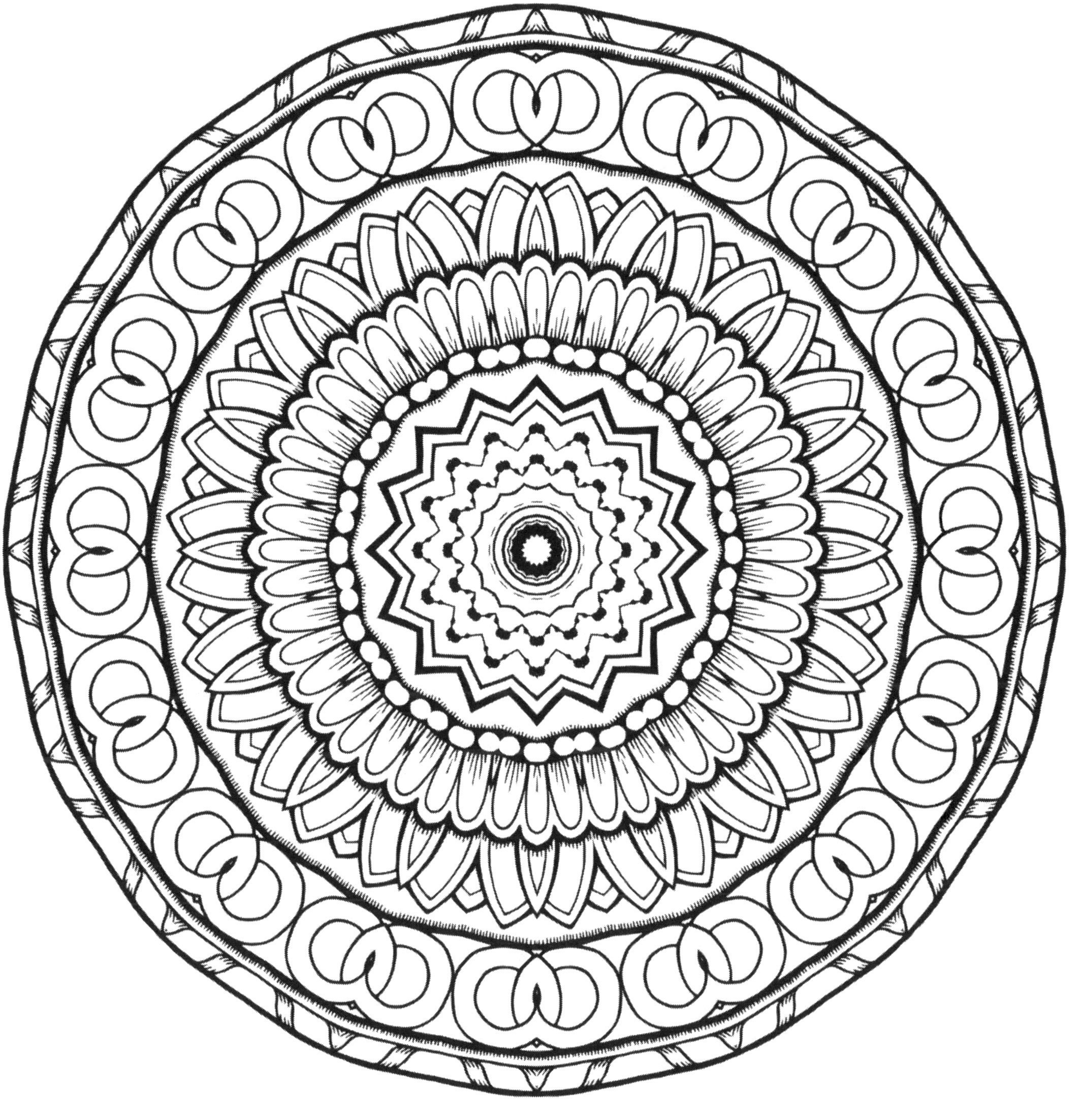

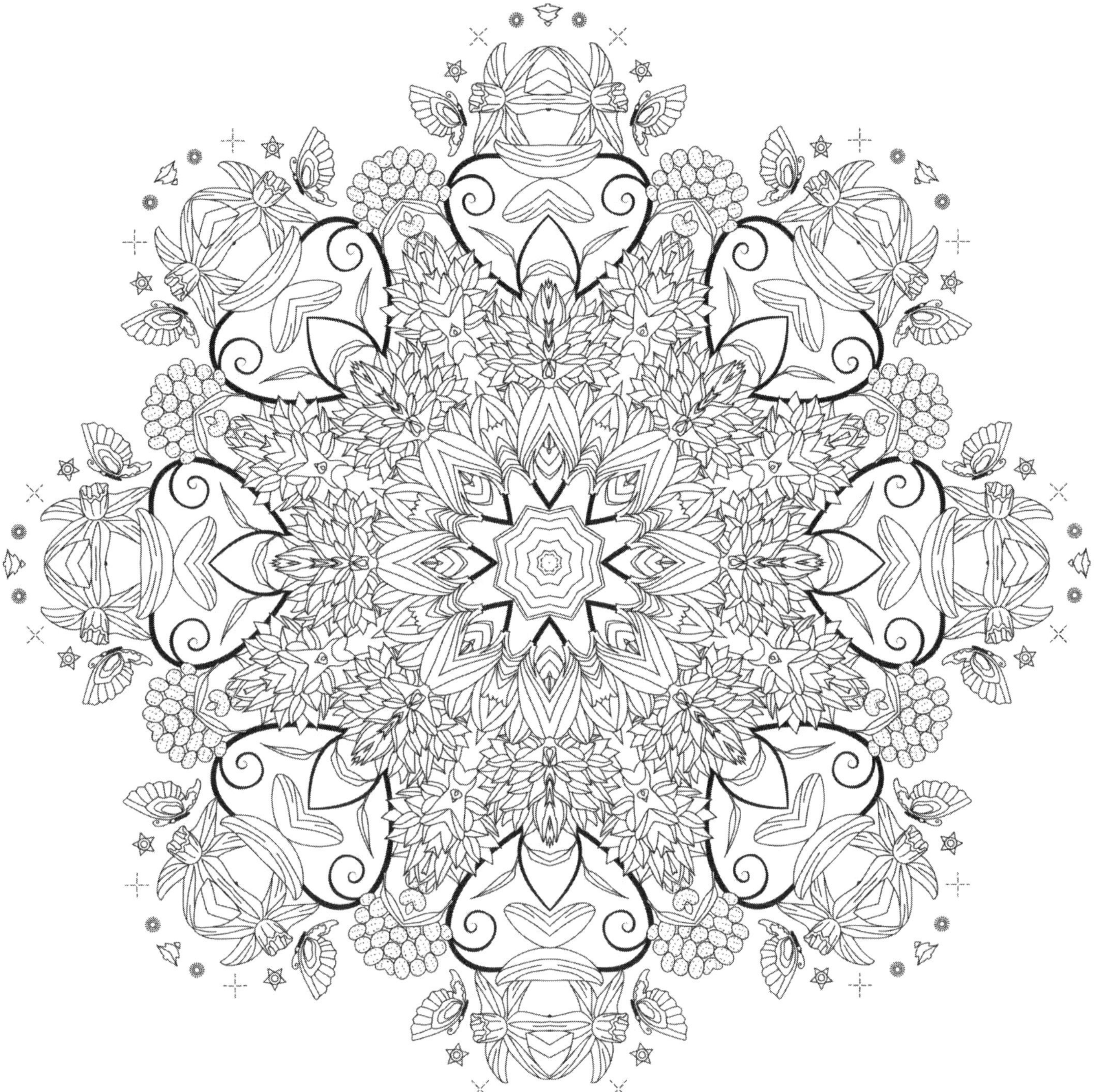

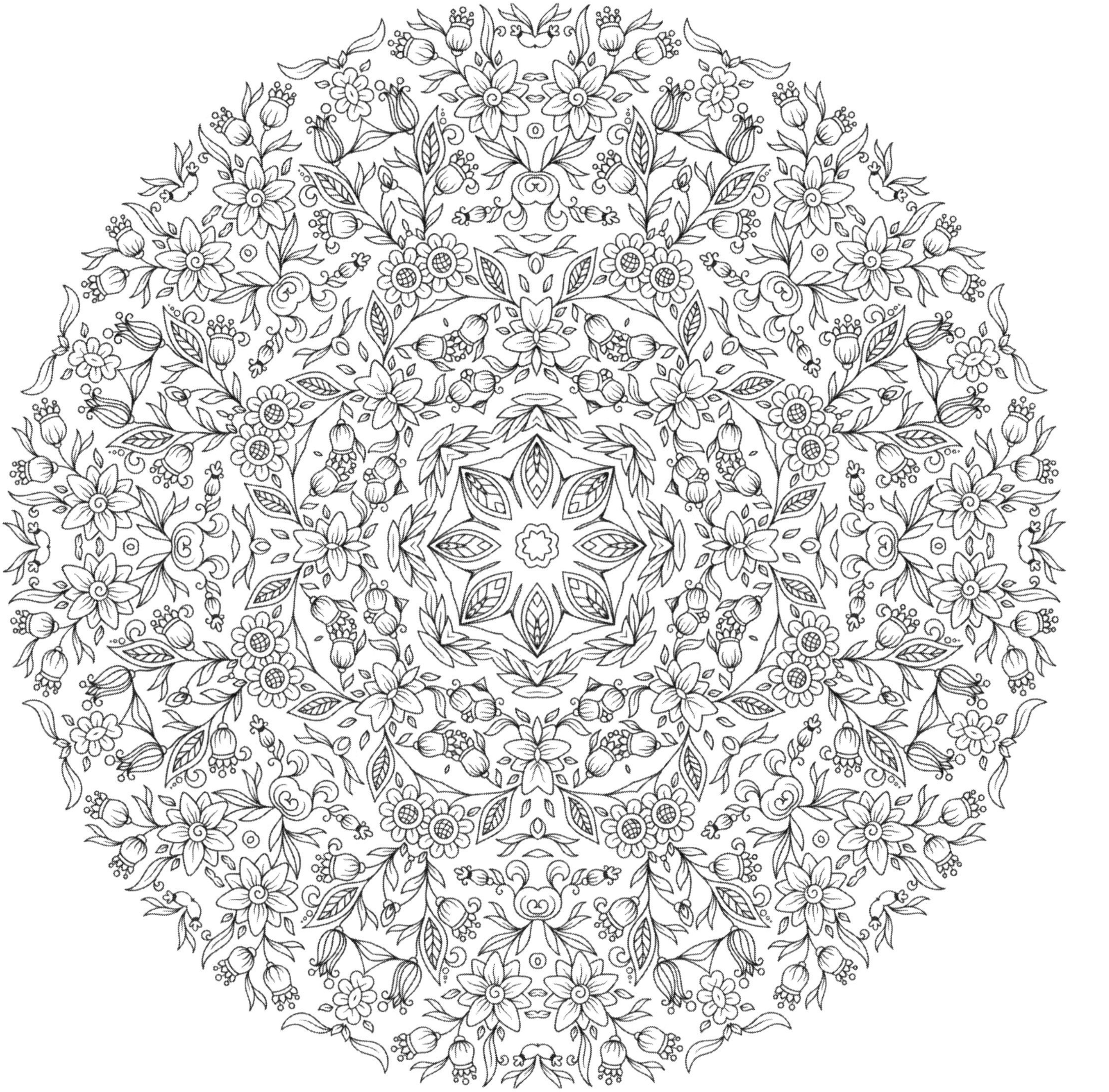

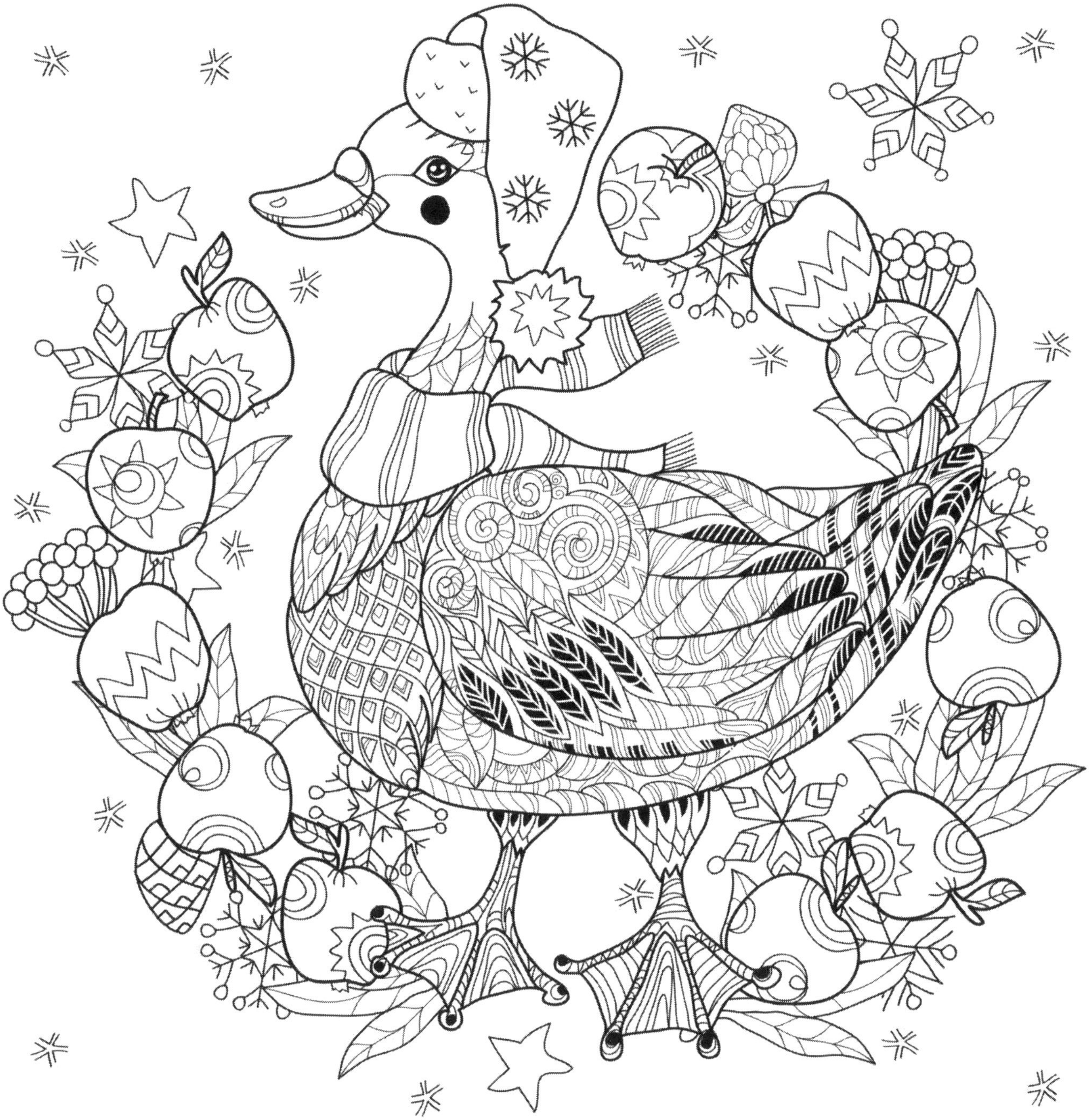

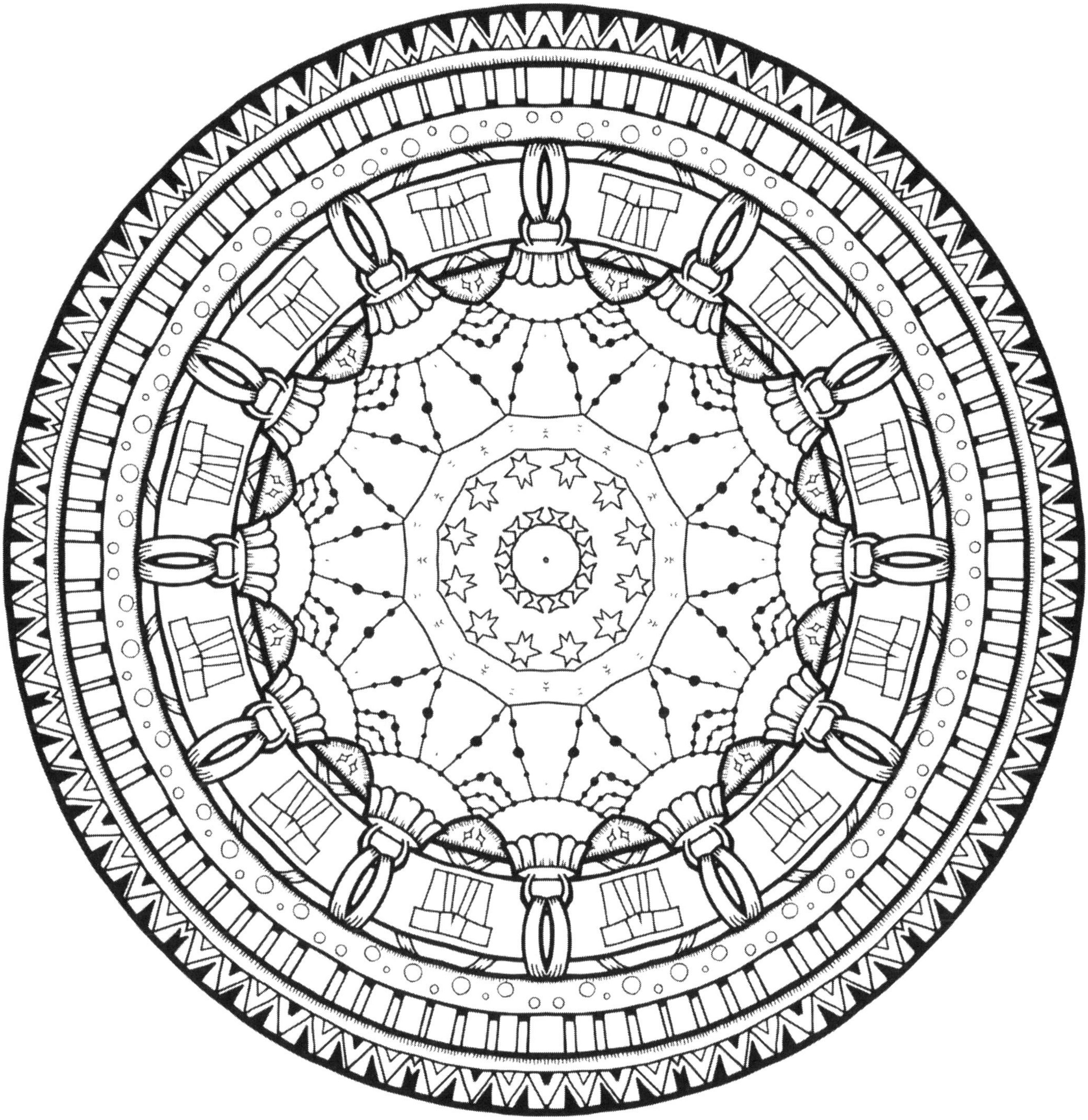

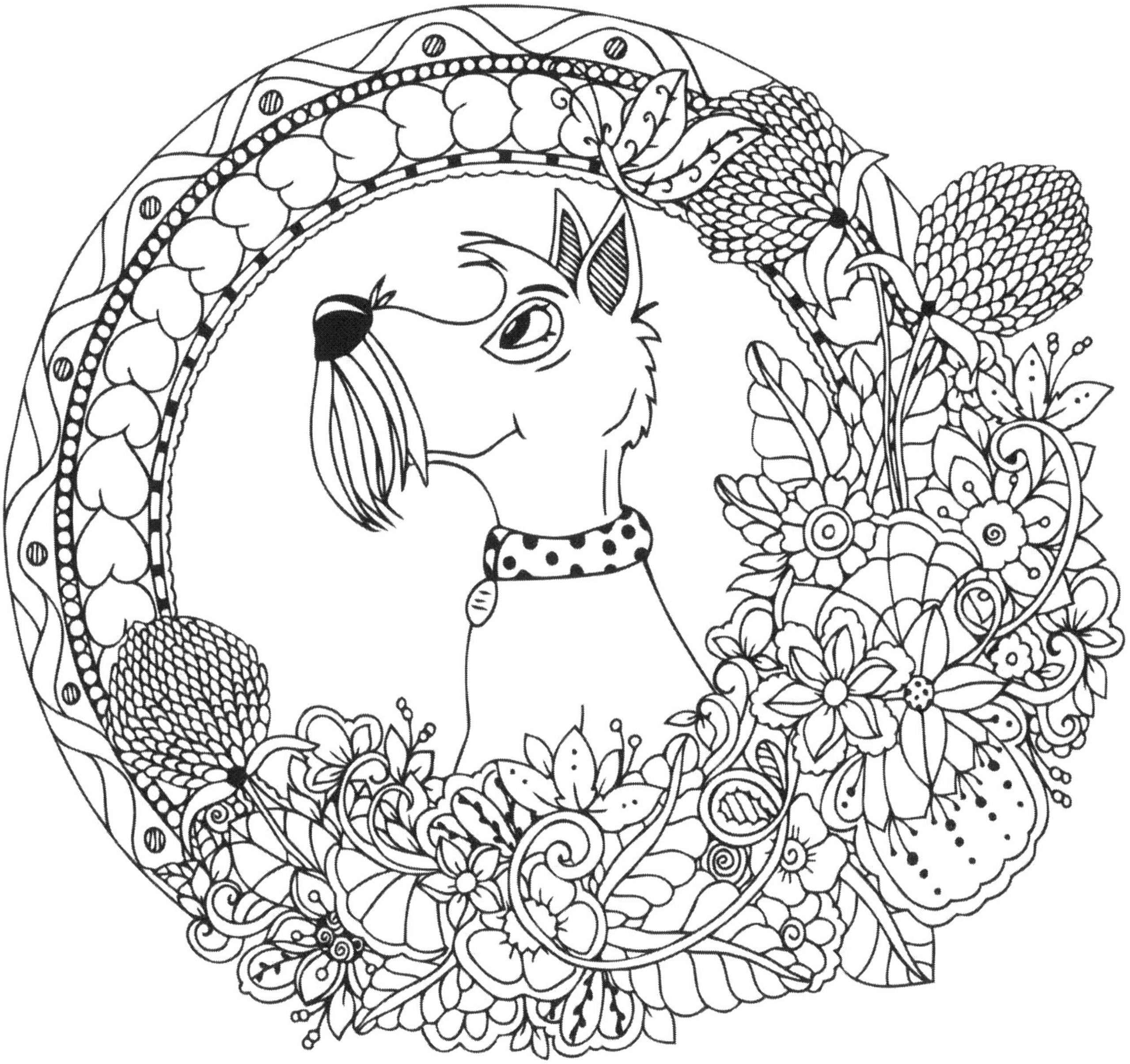

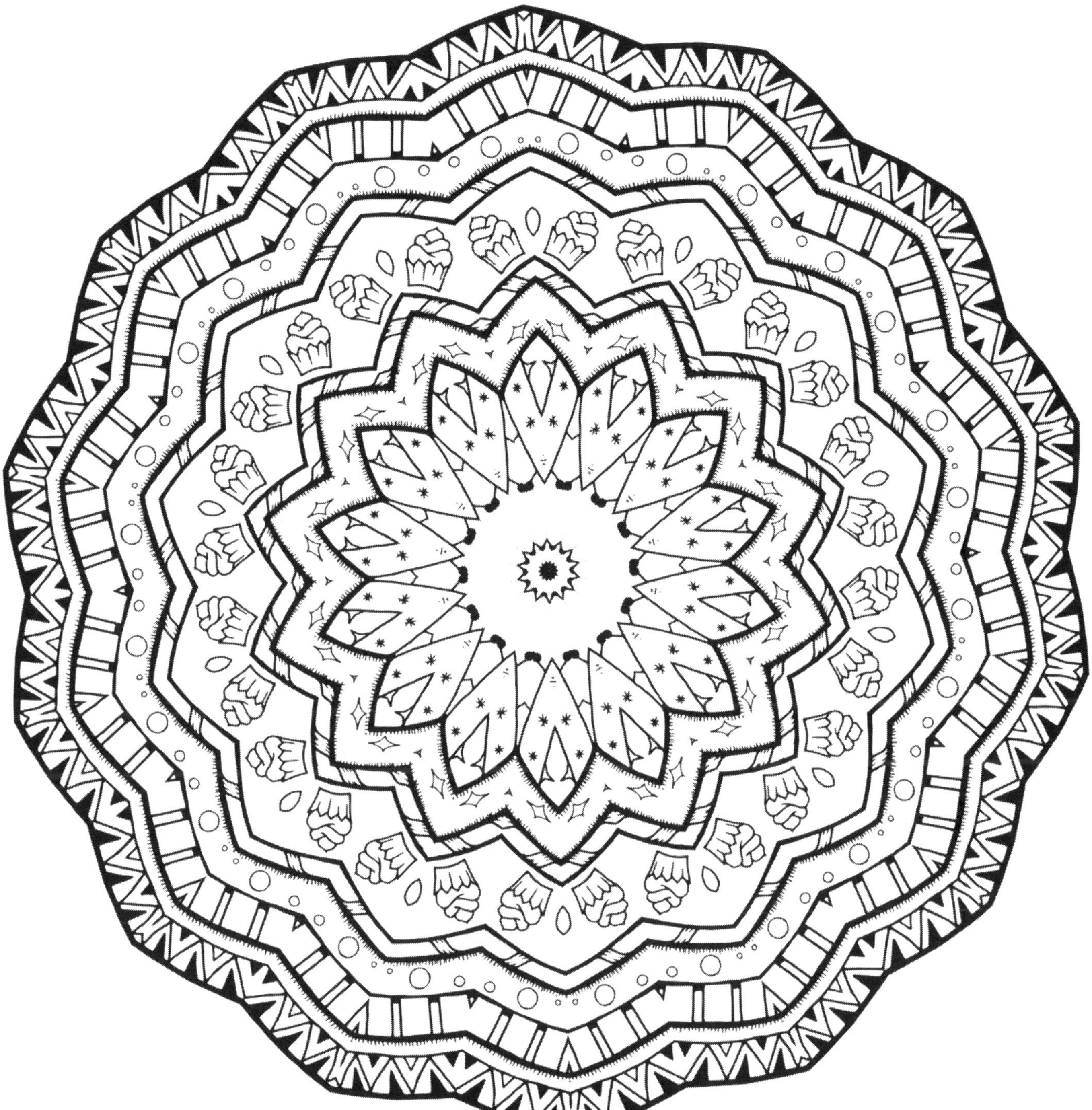

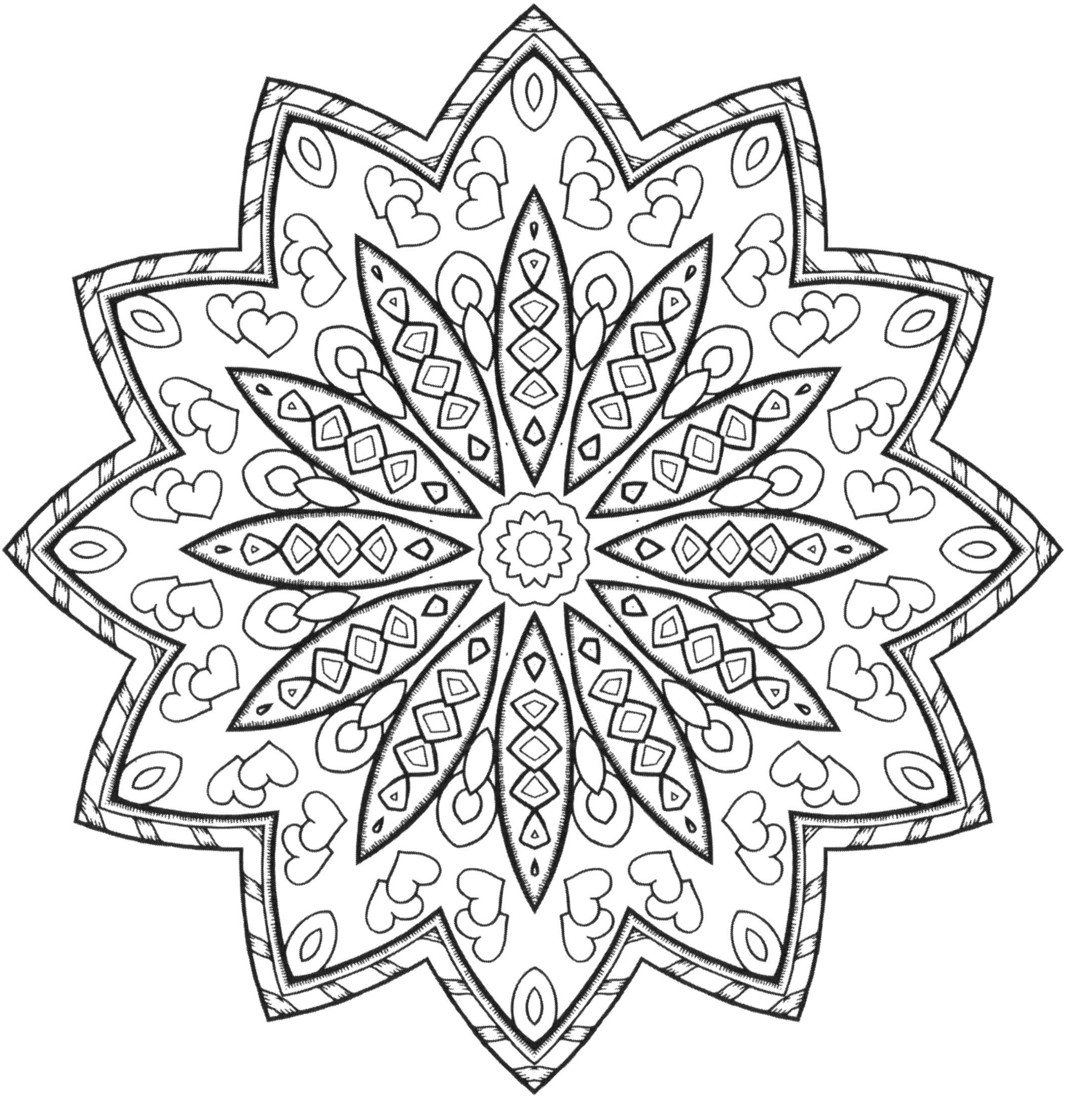

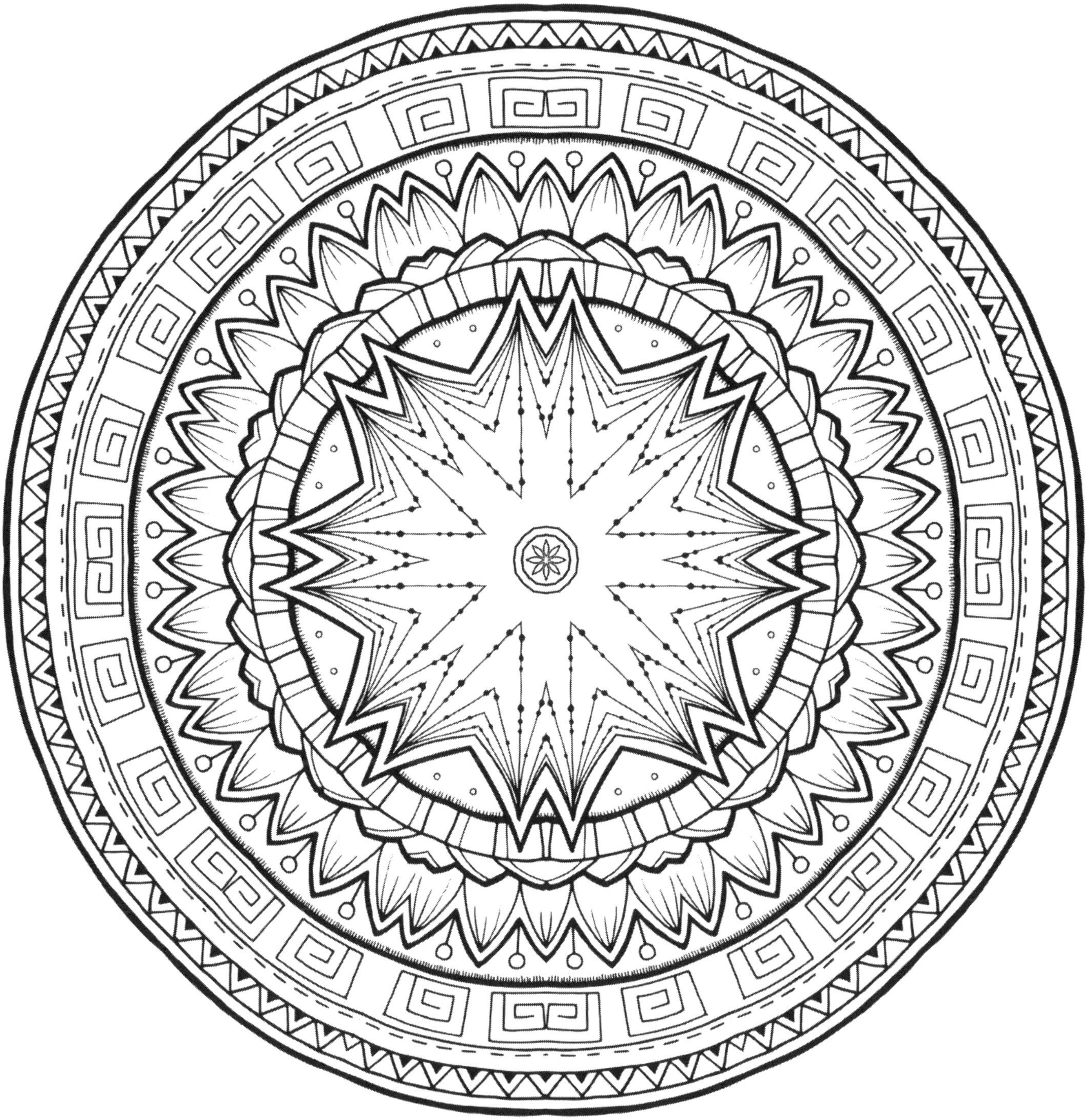

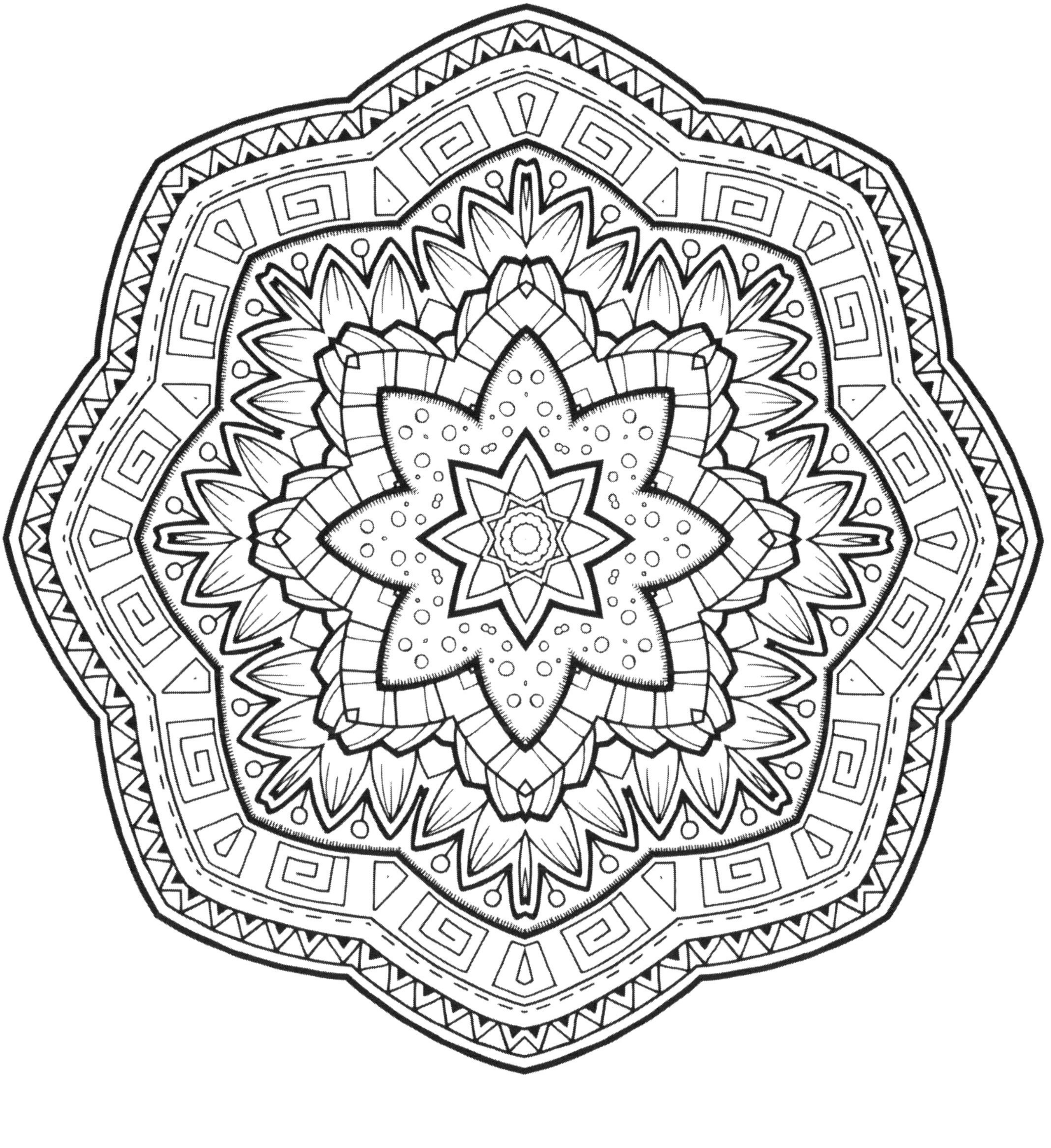

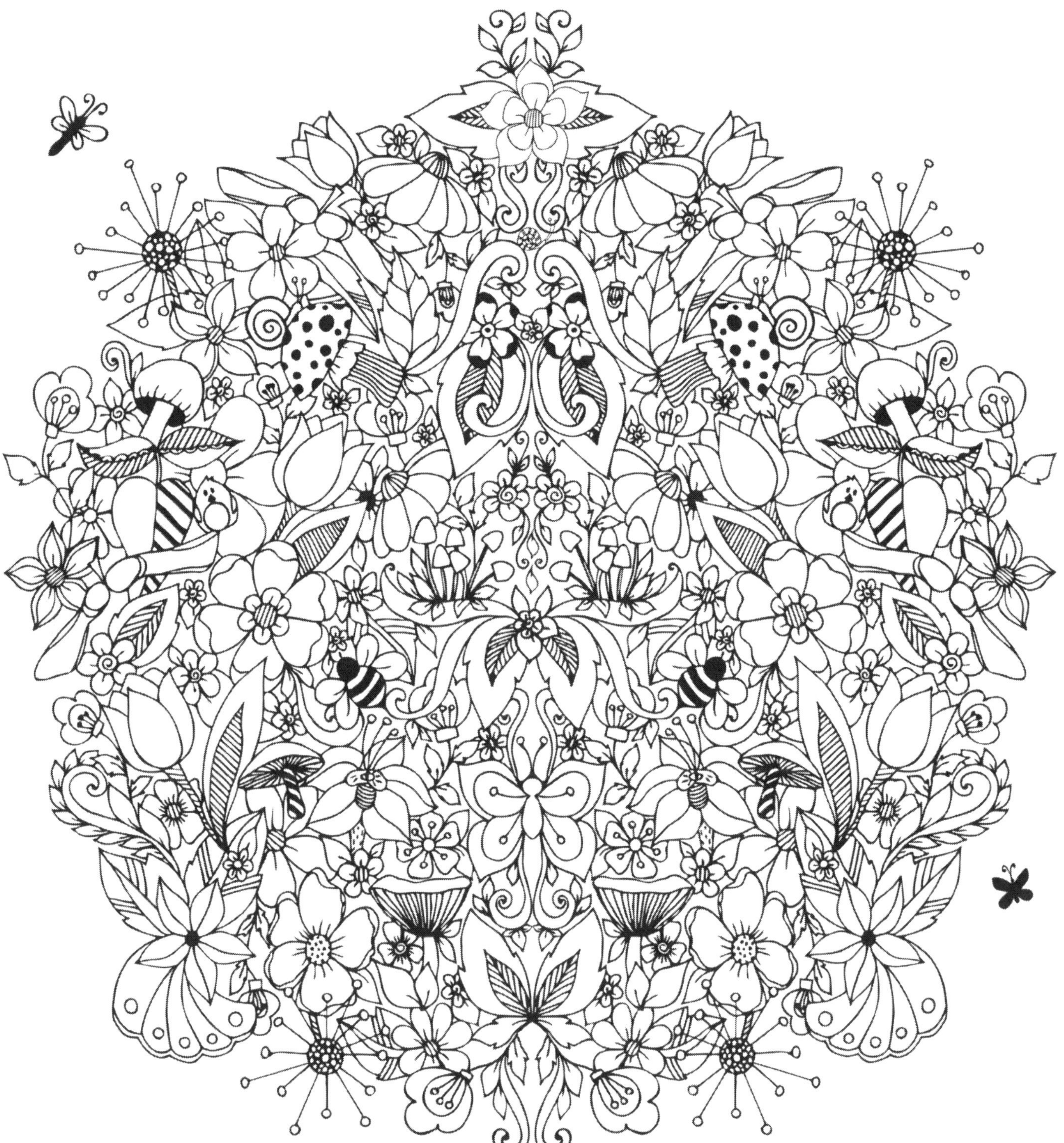

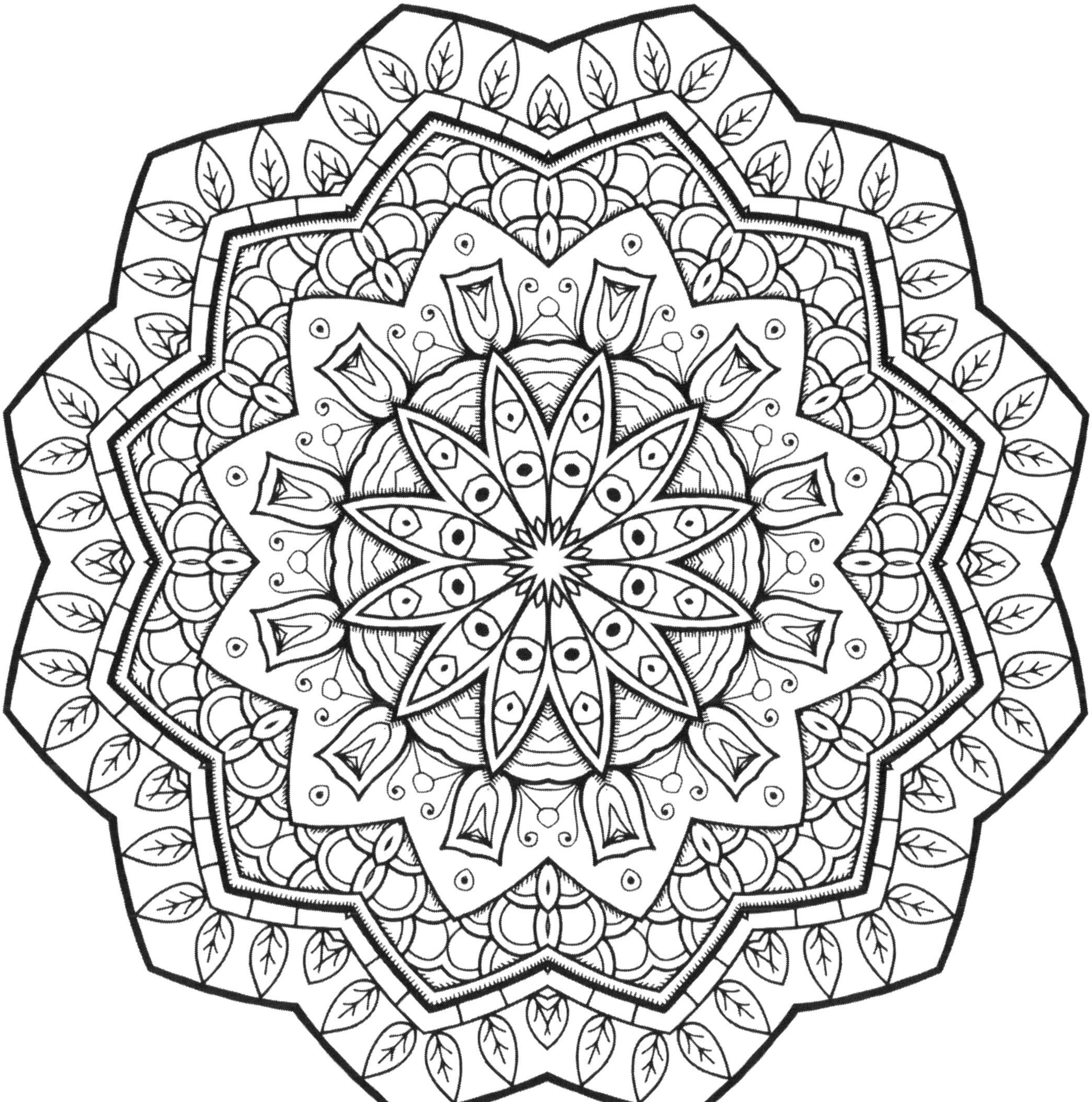

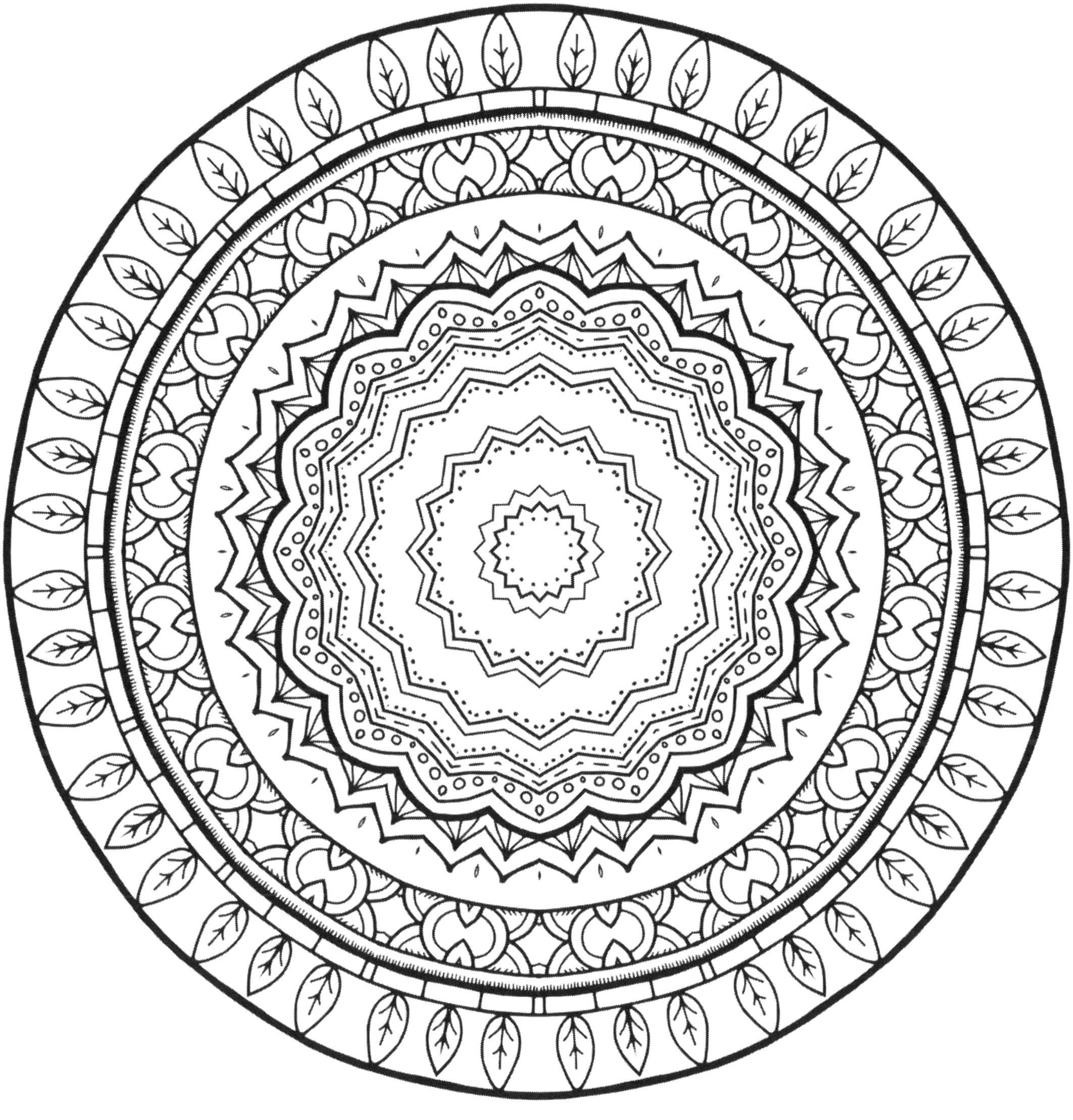

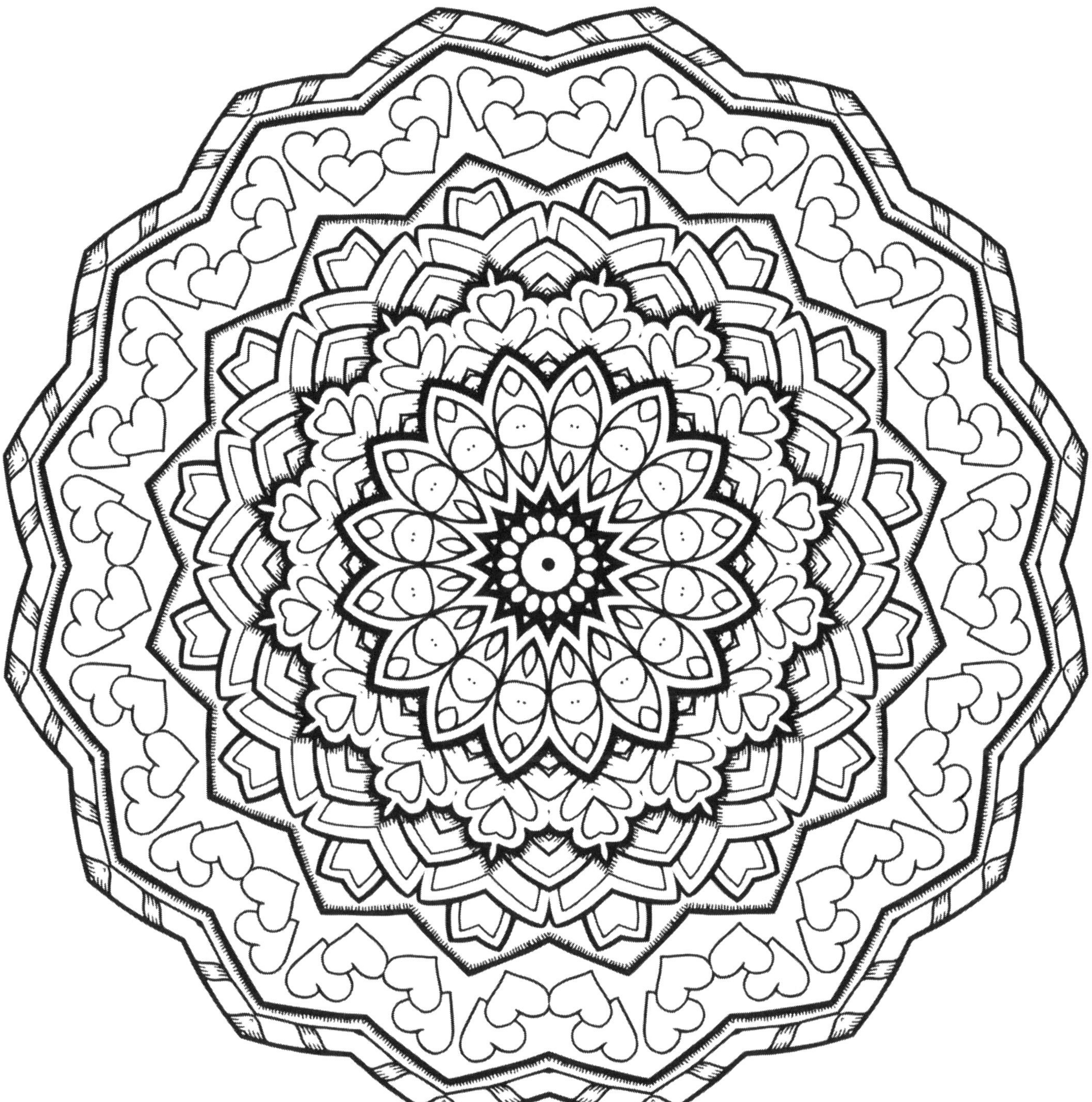

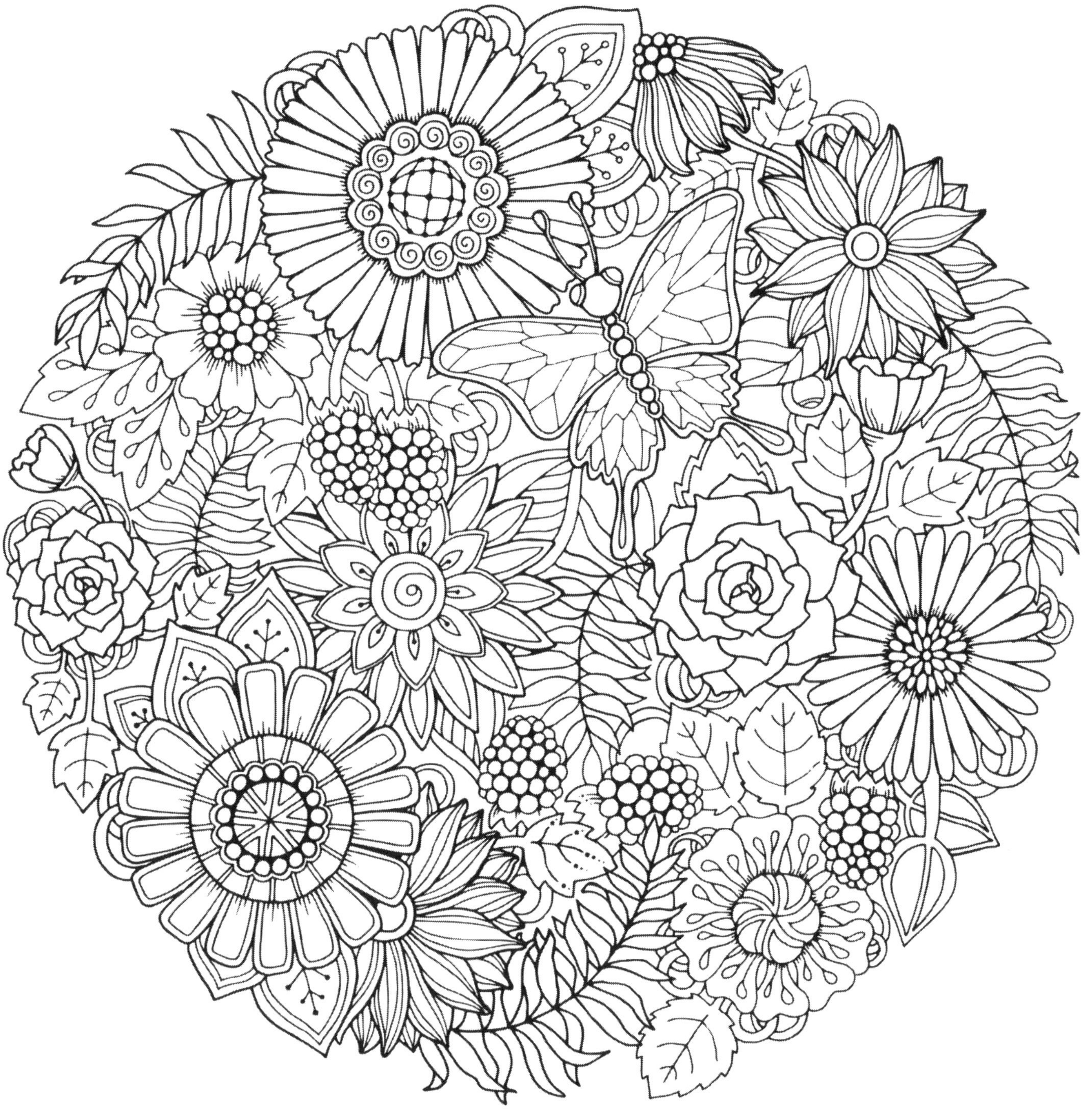

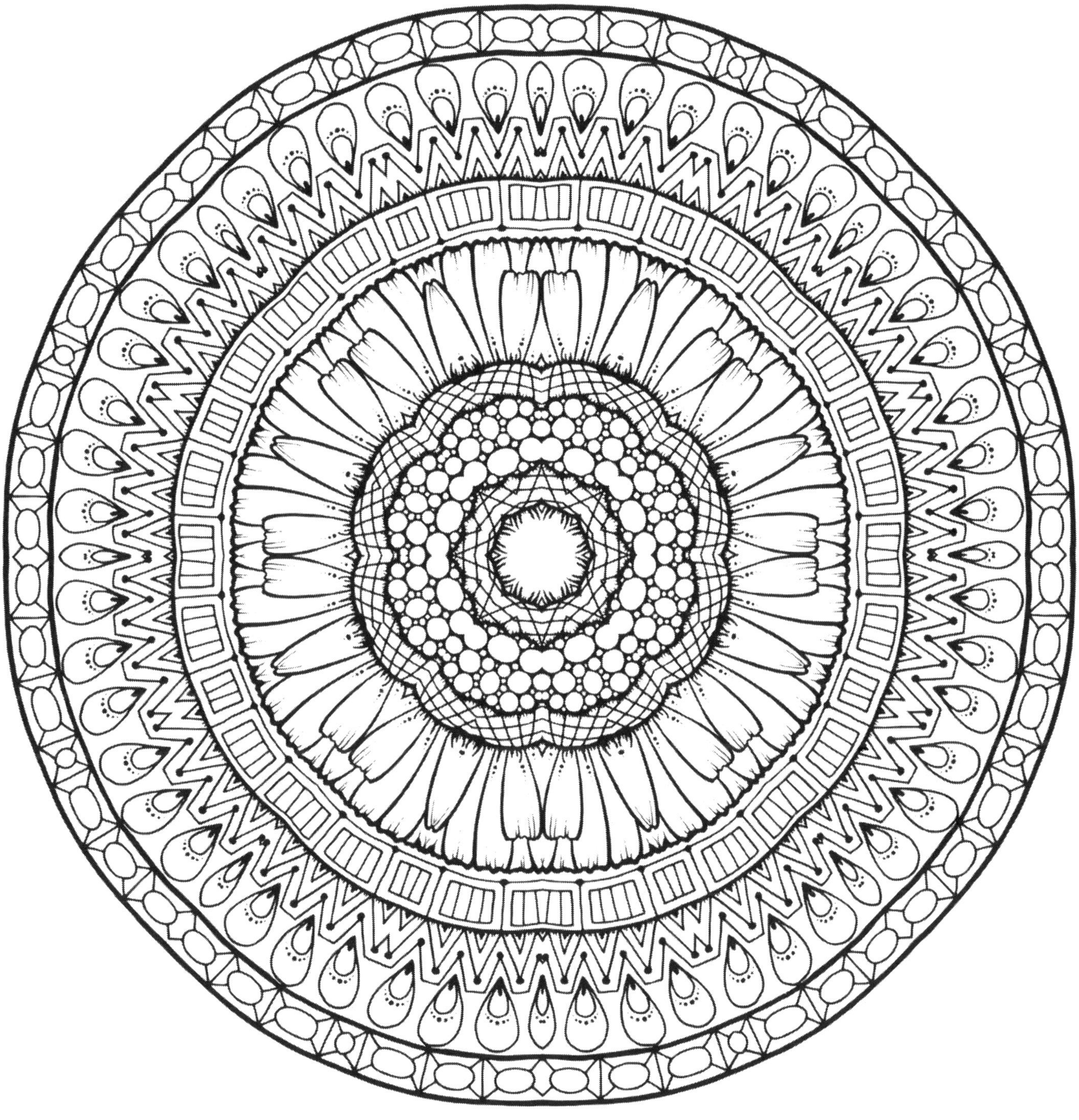

Made in the USA
Columbia, SC
02 December 2020

25877537R00043